THE BOARD-SAVVY SUPERINTENDENT

PAUL HOUSTON
AND
DOUG EADIE

A ScarecrowEducation Book
Published in partnership with the
American Association of School Administrators

The Scarecrow Press, Inc.
Lanham, Maryland, and Oxford
2002

A SCARECROWEDUCATION BOOK
Published in partnership with
the American Association of Scool Administrators

Published in the United States of America
by Scarecrow Press, Inc.
A Member of the Rowman & Littlefield Publishing Group
4720 Boston Way, Lanham, Maryland 20706
www.scarecroweducation.com

PO Box 317
Oxford
OX2 9RU, UK

British Library Cataloguing in Publication Information Available

Library of Congress Cataloging-in-Publication Data

Eadie, Douglas C.
    The board-savvy superintendent / Doug Eadie and Paul Houston.
        p. cm.
    "A ScarcroweEducation book."
    ISBN 0-8108-4470-2 (pbk. : alk. paper)
    1. School superintendents—United States. 2. School
board-superintendent relationships—United States. 3. School management
and organization—United States. I. Houston, Paul. II. Title.
    LB2831.72 .E23 2002
    371.2'011—dc21
                                                          2002008701

∞™ The paper used in this publication meets the minimum requirements of
American National Standard for Information Sciences—Permanence of Paper
for Printed Library Materials, ANSI/NISO Z39.48-1992.
Manufactured in the United States of America.

CONTENTS

FOREWORD

Paul Houston and Doug Eadie have written a powerful little book that is must reading for school board members, superintendents, and senior administrators aspiring to head their own school district some day. *The Board-Savvy Superintendent* is not another ho-hum summary of the governance literature that merely packages the conventional wisdom in a fancier wrapper. On the contrary, Paul and Doug have written a hard-hitting, nononsense "survive-and-thrive" manual that will help school district leaders succeed in these extraordinarily challenging times. Nor is *The Board-Savvy Superintendent* an attempt to fashion new governance theory. Rather, Paul and Doug have written a very practical, nuts-and-bolts guidebook that capitalizes on their hands-on experience in working with hundreds of boards and chief executive officers (CEOs) over the past quarter-century. The book's intended impacts are simple but ambitious: *The Board-Savvy Superintendent* should serve as a very practical resource in strengthening the governance of school districts, in building effective board–superintendent relationships, and in enriching the professional lives of superintendents.

Paul and Doug rightly recognize that the long-term success of public school districts in translating their educational visions into actual results depends not just on financial resources, dedicated and capable faculty, sound administration, and active parental involvement, but also on the kind of "high-impact" governance that really makes a difference in district affairs. They are also correct in recognizing that high-impact board leadership is buttressed by twin pillars: first, a "board-savvy" superintendent who is firmly committed to—and possesses the knowledge and skills to promote—strong governance, and second, a close, cohesive, and enduring board–superintendent "strategic leadership team."

Although *The Board-Savvy Superintendent* is chock-full of practical wisdom that can be put to immediate use in school districts, I was most impressed by Paul's and Doug's fresh look at the work of governing. They demystify the process, taking it out of the realm of policy making, thereby helping superintendents help their boards become more capable at governing. Paul and Doug describe governing in very practical terms as making decisions about very concrete governing "products" (such as values, vision, and mission) that help to determine where a school district should be headed, what it should be all about right now, and how well it is performing. One of the most important roles of the board-savvy superintendent, according to Paul and Doug, is to make sure that the board structure and process required to make these decisions is put in place.

I also found their advice for involving the board in leading strategic change a refreshing departure from conventional long-range planning, which has chewed up so many trees to produce so little of note over the past fifty years. Disdaining the traditional approach of merely projecting everything a school district is already doing into the future for an arbitrary and meaningless period, such as three or five years, Paul and Doug provide detailed, practical guidance for engaging the board creatively and proactively in a much more selective, vision-driven process that actually results in the implementation of strategic change. I agree with the authors that leading strategic change is, indeed, the "gold standard" for board leadership, and the truly board-savvy superintendents must be experts in the process.

I wholeheartedly recommend *The Board-Savvy Superintendent* to you. Its informal, plain-spoken style makes it an enjoyable read, and, more importantly, you will find it a rich resource that you can put to practical use in leading your district.

Anne L. Bryant, Executive Director
National School Boards Association
Alexandria, Virginia

PREFACE

HIGH STAKES

Our primary purpose in writing *The Board-Savvy Superintendent* is to provide you—as a school system superintendent or an executive aspiring to fill the top job in your school district—with detailed, practical, and thoroughly tested guidance for becoming what we call "board-savvy." Making the effort to become truly board-savvy is an extraordinarily high-stakes matter. It will be critically important to your professional and career development, to your board's success as a governing body, and to your district's effectiveness in these changing, challenging times.

Our experience over the past quarter-century—as teachers, executives, and consultants—has taught us that if you are truly a board-savvy superintendent, you are far more likely to survive and thrive as the CEO of your school district. We will, by the way, frequently refer to the superintendent of a school district as the CEO, for two reasons. First, "CEO" is universally used to describe the highest-ranking full-time professional who is hired by and reports to the board of an organization. Second, the superintendents in our experience who are most successful at working with their boards think of themselves as full-fledged CEOs. We well understand, however, that superintendents are more constrained in carrying out their CEO roles than for-profit CEOs, who for the most part are not as hemmed in by state regulation, court decisions, and highly involved boards.

Being board-savvy will equip you to build the kind of close, positive board–CEO "strategic leadership team" on which your district's educational and political success will depend. The true bottom-line result of this strong leadership, of course, is heightened school district performance that more fully meets the changing educational needs of your community.

If becoming truly board-savvy were a natural outcome of climbing the professional ladder in school districts, we would not have needed to write this book. However, we have learned from long experience that you can move step-by-step from the classroom through various administrative positions, eventually making it to the top spot in your district without acquiring the knowledge and skills that will ensure a strong board–superintendent strategic leadership team. Indeed, this understates the case, since we have met many superintendents over the years who, when they first sat in the CEO's seat in their district, knew virtually nothing about how to go about building a strong working relationship with their board.

This lack of knowledge has produced needless pain and suffering, professionally speaking. Countless times over the years we have encountered bright, dedicated, experienced superintendents with dissatisfied, frustrated, and even angry boards that, all too often, have dealt with their frustration by severing the relationship with the superintendent. One thing we know for sure is that no board in human history has been known to blame itself for its underperformance as a governing body or for the concomitant dissatisfaction that poor performance breeds; as your district's chief executive, you will always be your board's handiest culprit and—in too many cases—victim, if you are not board-savvy.

CORE ASSUMPTIONS

Our aim is not to examine board-savviness from a theoretical perspective. On the contrary, we want to arm you with very down-to-earth counsel in becoming a board-savvy CEO, drawing on our fifty-some years of accumulated experience. Three core assumptions are at the heart of *The Board-Savvy Superintendent*:

1. School districts sorely need the high-impact board leadership that is the acid test of whether you, as a superintendent, are really board-

savvy. The old-time passive-reactive school board that merely responds to finished staff work cannot provide the leadership that the times demand: in making truly strategic decisions, in selecting key district innovation targets, in monitoring district educational and administrative performance, and in building district ties to the wider community.

2. As the chief executive officer of your district, you are primarily accountable for—and the prime mover of—your school board's developing the capacity to produce "high-impact" governance that really makes a difference in your district's affairs. Your board certainly shares accountability for its own governing performance, but it would be totally unrealistic to expect your board members, as part-time unpaid volunteers, to take the lead in developing their governing capacity.

3. Your becoming a board-savvy superintendent involves your bringing the right attitude to your work with your board, as well as acquiring in-depth knowledge and skills in the governance realm. Board-savvy superintendents treat their board as a precious asset to be fully deployed in leading their districts—not as a damage-control challenge. They are passionately committed to strong board leadership, they make governance one of the highest-priority chief executive concerns, and they take the trouble to become experts in the nuts and bolts of board leadership.

WHAT FOLLOWS

The Board-Savvy Superintendent consists of five chapters:

Chapter 1: The Board-Savvy Superintendent in a Nutshell

Presents contemporary views of governance and CEOship that are key to your being board-savvy, explores the attitudinal dimension of board-savviness, and takes a close look at the technical skills that you must acquire to be board-savvy.

Chapter 2: Updating Your Board's Governing Design

Examines high-impact governance in detail and describes how you, as your district's CEO, can play an active, leading role in helping your board to update its governing design in order to produce high-impact governance: its role, work, and committee structure.

Chapter 3: Involving Your Board in Leading Strategic Change

Defines strategic change, examines the fatal flaws of the traditional comprehensive long-range planning process, describes a powerful new tool for producing significant district innovation—the Strategic Change Portfolio, and provides detailed counsel for involving your board creatively and proactively in one of the most important functions making up high-impact governance.

Chapter 4: Keeping the Board-Superintendent Partnership Healthy

Provides you with detailed guidance in maintaining a close, positive, productive working partnership with your board, focusing on eight critical elements of a successful relationship building and maintenance strategy, with special attention to one of the preeminent responsibilities of a high-impact governing board: board evaluation of CEO performance.

Chapter 5: Keeping Up with Your Reading

Identifies reliable sources of information on governance and the board–superintendent partnership and discusses selected recent books in the field.

ACKNOWLEDGMENTS

Although we wrote *The Board-Savvy Superintendent*, we cannot alone take credit for the practical wisdom that we share in this book. The lessons that we teach were learned through our work over the past twenty-five years with thousands of nonprofit and public board members and CEOs, who are in a very meaningful sense our coauthors. Tom Koerner, editorial director, and Cindy Tursman, acquisitions editor, at Scarecrow Education provided us with invaluable encouragement and support, as did Judy Seltz, associate executive director, Constituent Relations and Services, and Sherri Montgomery, executive assistant to the executive director, at the American Association of School Administrators. And coauthor Doug Eadie could not possibly have carried his fair share of the writing burden without the extraordinary support of his colleague and wife, Barbara Krai, who single-handedly managed their relocation from Dallas to the Tampa Bay area as this book was being written.

1

THE BOARD-SAVVY
SUPERINTENDENT
IN A NUTSHELL

RICH RETURN ON YOUR INVESTMENT

Investing your time and energy in becoming a board-savvy superintendent will produce rich dividends over time—for your school district and for you, professionally. Three sure signs of a board-savvy superintendent at work are, first, a school board that consistently produces what we call high-impact governance; second, a close, positive, and productive board–superintendent working partnership; and third, a school board that takes deep satisfaction in—and feels strong ownership of—its governing work:

- High-impact governing boards make a real difference through their governing activities, setting clear strategic directions to guide your district's development, fashioning policies that provide boundaries for current operations, rigorously monitoring short-term educational, administrative, and financial performance, evaluating longer-term educational effectiveness, and building close, positive ties with key stakeholders in your community. Your school district needs—and will benefit from—the leadership of a high-impact governing board.
- You and your school board are the two most important members of what we call your district's "strategic leadership team," whose continuous, close, creative collaboration is essential in areas that are critical for your district's long-term success: strategic planning, policy formulation,

goal setting, and public relations, to name but a few of the more important leadership functions. Neither partner making up the strategic leadership team can go it alone. The old-fashioned concept of your board's doing its own thing in the "policy" realm and you alone executing policies never corresponded to reality; and worse, this outdated notion has helped to erode many board–superintendent relationships. Not only do you, as your district's chief executive officer, need input from your board in making complex, high-stakes decisions involving significant long-term impacts, but you also need the legitimacy, authority, and support of your board in carrying out these decisions. And, of course, your board depends heavily on your detailed planning and management in carrying out its directions and policies. We—not we–they—is at the heart of effective district leadership.

- A satisfied board is one of the most important indications of a board-savvy CEO at work, and your job security as the CEO of your district depends heavily on your board members' satisfaction. You should never forget that school board members are human beings of a very special ilk: typically prominent, high-achieving members of your community who bring years of experience, wide networks, and considerable, diverse expertise to your district's boardroom. Their satisfaction depends on their making a significant difference in their governing work, on their feeling like the real owners of their decisions, and on having their normal ego needs met. Board-savvy superintendents pay close attention to seeing that this satisfaction is achieved and sustained.

HIGH COST OF BEING UN-SAVVY

Although not wanting to accentuate the negative, we feel obliged to point out that the cost of your not becoming board-savvy can be forbiddingly high. For one thing, your board will surely be less effective at doing its preeminent job: governing your district. In practice, this means that the vision and strategic directions that provide the framework for future development will be less clear, or even nonexistent, exacting a steep price over the long run in reduced educational effectiveness. Tough strategic decisions intended to deal with complex, high-stakes issues, such as whether to go for a new tax levy for badly needed capital improvements to make up for years of costly neglect, will not get made, will be poorly made, or will not be supported once they are made.

If you are not sufficiently board-savvy, the resulting lower-impact governing role of your board will inexorably erode your always fragile working partnership with the board, consequently reducing your effectiveness as your district's CEO and inevitably damaging the morale of administrators and faculty. Public bickering between you and your board is likely to increase, not only exhausting you emotionally but also jeopardizing your district's reputation and credibility in the eyes of the public-at-large. Ultimately, your very job will be put at risk, and should the divorce eventually come, you will not be the sole victim; your district will have to go through the almost always traumatic process of finding someone to replace you.

Yes, the price of your not becoming truly board-savvy is potentially high enough to make doing so one of your highest priorities as a CEO and, indeed, an ethical obligation.

A WORD ON THE FIELD OF GOVERNANCE

Before turning to the characteristics of board-savvy superintendents and how you can go about becoming more board-savvy, we want to briefly look at the very complex, dramatically changing field called governance. You might be surprised to learn that, even though nonprofit and public boards have been a prominent feature of the American organizational landscape for well over a century, the subject of board leadership has only in recent years received detailed attention. Even today, it is safe to say, the books dealing with executive leadership probably outnumber books dealing with the work of boards one hundred to one, and you will be fortunate to find—after a lengthy search—more than five or six books on governance in a major bookstore anywhere in the country.

We think the reason for this traditional neglect of governance as a subject probably has to do with the fact that serving on a board is, by definition, a part-term, amateur "business." Boards are populated by lay people who are not expected to be experts in the business being governed, whether education, health services, or regional planning. By contrast, executive management is the work of full-time professionals who are expected to be—and respected as—real experts. Becoming a top professional and an expert is obviously a challenging task; anybody can serve on a board (or so the traditional view has it).

The most important consequence of this lack of serious attention to the work of governing until recently has been the failure of board "organizational development." Of course, boards are by definition organizations within the wider organization of which they are a part, just like an office of curriculum and instruction or an office of the district superintendent. They are a permanently established group of people working through formal structure and process to achieve a valid mission: to govern. Traditionally, empty descriptions of boards as "policy-making" bodies have substituted for serious development of their organizational role, governing work, and governing structure.

To add insult to injury, not only has the work of boards traditionally been neglected as a subject, but much of the so-called governance literature reflects a narrow administrative control bias. As a consequence, what we call the "passive-reactive" approach to board leadership has reigned supreme until recent years. The passive-reactive board basically responds to finished staff work coming from the CEO and senior managers; above all else it judges, rather than proactively directs, and its role in shaping such strategic products as a vision statement or set of long-range growth targets tends to be slight. The passive-reactive board is essentially a high-level audience, and its work all too often consists of thumbing through tomes, rather than guiding and shaping important decisions.

The administrative control perspective has also spawned a number of what we call "fallacious little golden rules" that you will follow at your peril. One of the most notorious is that small boards are more effective at governing than larger ones. Have you ever asked why this is the case? If you think about it, you can see that the only rationale is administrative efficiency, undergirded by a clear damage-control bias (as in "the board is a real pain in the posterior capable of causing trouble, so a smaller board is without question preferable to a larger one"). On reflection, however, a larger, more diverse board (up to some reasonable limit, say, fifteen to twenty-one) will enrich decision making by bringing in diverse viewpoints and perspectives based on wider experience and expertise. Not employing committees is another one of those unreliable little golden rules; in reality, well-designed committees, as we will discuss later, can be a powerful mechanism for in-depth board member involvement in the process of governing.

And one of the most notorious bits of advice is to send your board "fin-ished" staff work. This might make sense in those instances when there is no room for serious board involvement (such as a slew of employment con-tracts, which should, indeed, be absolutely accurate and "finished"), but just keep in mind that when something going to a board is truly finished, there is literally no opportunity for creative board input and hence no opportunity to build board member feelings of ownership and satisfaction. We could cite other examples of thoughtless advice intended to limit board involvement in governing, but the point is made: understand the motivation and underlying rationale of any advice before taking it.

We are pleased to report that over the past decade or so, a much more pos-itive and dynamic board-governing model has emerged and been widely tested. In this model, governing is seen as a much more complex process than merely policy making (of course, policies are broad rules, and the business of fashioning and updating these rules cannot possibly keep a self-respecting board busy). Essentially, governing your school district is defined as:

> Playing the leading role in answering the three most important questions about your district: Where is your district headed over the long run (its vi-sion, strategic directions, and long-range goals)? What is your district now (its mission, operational goals, current resource allocation, etc.)? How is your dis-trict performing (educationally, administratively, financially)?

It is now recognized that developing a board's capacity to govern basically means to strengthen its capacity to answer these three preeminent questions, continuously and systematically. When we use the term "high-impact" gov-ernance, we mean doing an outstanding job of answering these questions.

THE BOARD-SAVVY SUPERINTENDENT AT WORK

The long-term benefits of your becoming board-savvy are, indeed, sub-stantial, and it makes the best of sense for you to invest in building your board-savviness. Assuming that you have decided to take our advice, you need to familiarize yourself with the traits that truly board-savvy CEOs demonstrate and how they work with and for their boards. We begin this tour of the board-savvy terrain with a look at two board-savvy superintendents in action—at the Hillsdale Consolidated School District and the Mt. Auburn City School District—and a classic case of a nonsavvy CEO at work at the Morningside Heights schools. Although the cases are fictional, be assured that they are based on numerous real-life examples that we have observed over the years.

Involving the Hillsdale School Board in Planning

Driving home Saturday afternoon after the second annual board–superintendent–executive team strategic work session ("retreat," in popular parlance), Dr. Ina Crawford, superintendent of the Hillsdale Consolidated School District, reflected on how far she and her board had come over the past two years in strengthening the board's leadership and building a really strong and cohesive board–superintendent partnership. "There's no question," she thought, "that beefing up the board's involvement in the district's planning process was the single most important step the board and I have taken as part of the district's 'Board Tune-Up Initiative.'" The board's playing a more creative and proactive role in district planning had yielded a powerful return to the district, not only in terms of clearer strategic directions, but also of board member satisfaction and the feeling of owning critical planning decisions. "Working with a satisfied, fully engaged board is day and night easier than where we were two years ago," Ina thought as she pulled into her driveway.

Two years earlier, Ina's working partnership with the Hillsdale board was badly frayed and growing worse by the day. The new board chair, Aaron Deas, and four other members of the nine-person board, having grown increasingly frustrated and irritated, were up in arms about the board's largely passive role in district planning, which, as one board member observed during a heated discussion after a board meeting, "makes us feel like we're an audience, not really leaders. Our job is apparently to thumb through well-crafted planning documents that are basically finished. We can ask questions, but if we try to make major changes, we're made to feel like we're meddling in Ina's business—kind of like barbarians at the gate. So we raise relatively minor questions that patently don't make a real difference in the scheme of things."

Initially thrown off balance by the vehemence of the criticism and feeling more than a little defensive, Ina at first felt like circling the wagons and fending off this attack on her executive prerogatives. After all, she'd always believed that one of the twenty-four-carat golden rules for educational administrators was to produce finished documents for the board that would stand up to the severest scrutiny. After all, wasn't that the sincerest form of respect for the board? "Finished staff work" was the mantra that she had heard repeated countless times as she climbed the ladder to the CEO's office.

Fortunately, Ina, although combative by nature and a jealous guardian of her CEO prerogatives, resisted her instinctive urge to do battle, deciding instead to try to understand where Aaron and the other critics on the board were coming from and to be open to creative solutions. It didn't take her long to see their point. Taking a close look at how the district was handling strategic planning, which—in theory anyway—was supposed to be the vehicle for board direction setting at the highest level, she realized how wide the gap between theory and practice was. The last time the "five-year educational plan of advancement" was updated, some five months ago, the district had employed a consultant to work with the executive team in updating long-range goals and mapping out broad strategies to achieve them.

Truth be told, the fifty-five-page document that went to the board was, indeed, largely finished, and the changes that were made over the course of three committee-of-the-whole work sessions were essentially cosmetic. Reflecting on the experience, Ina realized that her board hadn't made much of a difference, and if she had been in their place, she would have been pretty dissatisfied herself, and probably eventually angry as well.

Deciding to grab the proverbial bull by the horns, Ina asked Aaron to join her for lunch in a couple of days, and the first thing she said when they sat down was, "Aaron, I think you and the other critics on the board have a point in feeling pretty unhappy with the board's role in planning, and I'd like to propose a way to get things on the right track." Ina proposed that Aaron appoint an ad hoc committee of three board members with whom she and her associate superintendent for planning and development would work in coming up with a more creative and satisfying board role in planning, especially of the strategic ilk. The resulting game plan involved two key reforms that subsequently turned the situation completely around:

- First, the board agreed to create a standing committee, Planning and Development, that would be responsible for annually reaching agreement with Ina on the planning calendar—focusing on points of intensive board involvement—for designing (with Ina) and hosting special planning work sessions of the board, and for playing a hands-on role in shaping key strategic products, such as an updated district vision statement.
- Second, the board decided to participate in an annual one-and-one-half-day strategic work session to kick off the planning cycle. Involving the CEO and all members of her executive team, the session focused on revisiting the district's vision for the future, on identifying critical issues facing the district, and on brainstorming possible "change initiatives" to deal with the issues. The new planning and development committee is formally responsible for following up on the annual session, basically by working closely with Ina and her executive team in selecting the strategic issues demanding attention during the coming year and reviewing—and recommending to the full board—the change initiatives that staff developed to deal with the selected issues. For example, last year two initiatives topped the list: putting together an ultimately successful campaign to pass a tax levy for significant capital improvements and launching a school–community task force to deal with the dramatically increasing racial tension at Fernway Middle School.

"Thank heaven," Ina mused, as she poured a cup of coffee that Saturday afternoon after the second strategic work session, "I had the good sense to work with Aaron and the other board members in beefing up their planning work. Opening up the planning process to more creative board involvement went against my gut instinct and what I was taught coming up the ladder, but it's sure paid dividends." Not only, by the way, had Ina actively and creatively collaborated with the board in redesigning the planning process, she had also taken the trouble to familiarize herself with contemporary thinking in the field of strategic planning, which, she learned, had moved well beyond old-time comprehensive long-range planning. Ina had also prepared herself for her planning work with her board by seeking out real-life examples of creative, substantive, and satisfying school board involvement in planning that might provide her and the board with a model of sorts to follow.

Evaluating the Mt. Auburn Superintendent

"Whew," Hal Marshall thought, "that was really grueling, but well worth it. I'm sure glad that I pushed the board to take evaluation of my performance as superintendent more seriously, rather than just having everyone fill out another one of those functional questionnaires like we used to do every year or so. What's really made a difference is homing in on what board members expect from me in supporting their governing work and getting down to brass tacks where there have been vague questions about how I'm doing."

Superintendent of the Mt. Auburn City School District for the past six years, Hal has done a bang-up job of strengthening the district as an educational enterprise, which is what he was hired to do. Real progress has been made on every front: senior SAT scores, the graduate college-going percentage, passing rates on the state exams, attendance, and parent involvement. Certainly the taxpayers must think good things are happening, having overwhelmingly approved the tax hike on the ballot last month.

So Hal has basically done what he's been hired to do, and for the first three years his relationship with the Mt. Auburn board appeared to be made in heaven, and he could do nothing wrong. But the past couple of years saw Hal's partnership with his board grow increasingly tense, which was frustrating because the annual evaluation questionnaire (a checklist format asking board members to rate the superintendent on a five-point scale in a number of functional areas, such as strategic planning, financial management, educational leadership, human resource management, public representation, etc.) didn't bring any problems to the surface. Things were clearly getting worse, but Hal could not pinpoint why.

Hal knew that he had to get to the bottom of the growing unhappiness with his leadership among board members—either that or update his curriculum vitae and begin to look for other opportunities, because the proverbial writing was clearly on the wall. He identified the superintendent evaluation process as a potentially powerful tool for relationship repair and rebuilding, even though it was obviously not serving that purpose well as currently practiced. As he thought about it, Hal realized that the challenge was to turn the evaluation process into a more meaningful tool by building into the process an agreement with the board on detailed superintendent performance targets on which a more objective evaluation could be based. These targets clearly had to go beyond the standard checklist of functional responsibilities to be of any use in maintaining the board–superintendent relationship

Having thought through the matter of evaluation, Hal raised the issue with his board chair, William Clay, at the next of their regular twice-a-month breakfast meetings. William, convinced that Hal had hit the right nail on the head, appointed three board members to serve on a superintendent evaluation committee, which was explicitly charged to reach agreement with Hal on the performance targets that would be the basis for the next evaluation. The process really did help to turn around a potentially deadly situation (for Hal, anyway). What's made the new evaluation process so powerful as a relationship maintenance tool is the concept of two-tiers of superintendent targets: first, overall district educational and administrative performance targets annually updated through the operational planning and budget development process, and, second, superintendent-specific targets relating to Hal's particular value-added as the district's CEO.

For example, the process involves Hal's negotiating specific performance targets in areas such as support for the board, external relations, and strategic planning. The danger of Hal's being criticized for failing to meet expectations that he never understood has gone down to virtually zero since the new process has been in place. To take a practical example, when Hal and the board committee responsible for his evaluation were discussing the superintendent's role in district external relations, he realized that board members expected him to actively support their involvement, not just his own. Subsequently, he has paid much more attention to making sure that his board members are regularly booked to speak before community groups and to participate in radio and TV talk shows.

The Less-Savvy Morningside Heights Superintendent

Angela Hopkins, superintendent of the Morningside Heights schools, was blessed with more than her share of calcium and must have ranked 9.5 out of

10 on the courageous leadership scale. Definitely not one to avoid bad news, she wasn't about to sit back, "fiddling while Rome burned." She wasn't afraid to tackle problems head-on, and she wasn't in the habit of mincing words in the process. And the news *was* bad, no question about it. The slow but steady decline in Morningside Heights's overall population, combined with a growing proportion of childless families in the community, spelled the doom of some of Morningside Heights's cherished neighborhood elementary schools. Enrollment had fallen dangerously low in three neighborhoods, sending per-pupil costs sky high, and all forecasts—by the city planning department, a local college, and the regional planning commission—promised more of the same. Action clearly needed to be taken. The choice was stark: either move in the direction of consolidation, eliminating two or three neighborhood elementary schools, or defend the rapidly escalating costs to the growing majority of homeowners without children in the school system.

In typical can-do fashion, Angela put together a staff task force to come up with a cost-reduction strategy. She informed her school board that she was launching the task force and that the board could expect her recommendations within the next four to five months. Angela retained a consulting firm to assist the task force in its deliberations and to write the final report to the board. Presented with a detailed charge, provided a thorough orientation on the process it would follow, and supported by a very capable consulting team, the task force did an exemplary job of homing in on the critical issues and examining from a rigorous cost/benefit perspective the district's cost-control options in the context of an apparently inexorable decline in neighborhood school enrollment. Although Angela periodically briefed the Morningside Heights board on progress in closed executive session, the content of the work was kept under wraps so that public controversy wouldn't be ignited.

Angela stayed close to the task force's work, holding five intensive work sessions with the group at which the recommendations were examined under a microscope to detect and correct errors in logic and fact. By the time the report was ready for board review, it was a beautifully crafted document that, with impeccable logic and a clear command of the issues, made a compelling case for consolidating five neighborhood schools into three over the next two years. Angela scheduled a special half-day board work session, at which she, the task force chair, and the senior member of the consulting team were to present the report and answer any questions board members had.

Angela, never one to leave loose ends, had also prepared a board resolution directing her to proceed with detailed implementation planning.

The work session was (predictably, in hindsight) a disaster, seriously fraying the board–superintendent relationship and sending it into a tailspin that could not be reversed in the coming months. By the time Angela had been forced out seven months later, the board was overseeing the work of a broad-based community task force that had been charged to come up with recommendations to deal with declining enrollment while preserving, to a feasible extent, the neighborhood schools. Who knows? Perhaps the same conclusions would have been reached, but too late for Angela. Once the emotional wounds had healed a bit, Angela was able to see clearly where she had erred: in not involving the board early enough in exploring options, in confronting them with a dramatic choice that felt politically dangerous with little warning, in presenting the report in plenary session without the intermediary step of involving an ad hoc committee of the board. Board ownership of the report was nil, meaning that commitment was minimal.

Angela paid a high price for being so un-board-savvy, but what is especially interesting about this case is that she was for the most part a highly capable CEO. She ensured that a technically superb job was done in dealing with the issue of declining enrollment in her district, and she submitted a top-notch report to her board. The lesson we want you to take away from this vignette is that you can do 99 percent of the CEO's job quite well and still pay a huge price for behaving in an un-board-savvy fashion in a particular instance.

A PROFILE OF BOARD-SAVVYNESS

A profile of the board-savvy superintendent emerges from the Hillsdale, Mt. Auburn, and Morningside Heights vignettes. These stories, which are drawn from our real-life experience, paint a picture of the board-savvy superintendent in terms of traits, technical skills, do's and don'ts. We learn that, above all else, the board-savvy superintendent:

- **Brings the Right Attitude to Working with the Board**
  The board-savvy superintendent sees his or her board as a precious asset that is to be fully deployed in leading the school district, rather than

as a damage-control challenge. He or she wants the board to be a high-impact governing body that realizes its tremendous leadership promise in practice and fervently believes in working in close partnership with the board.

- **Makes the Governance a Top Priority**
  The board-savvy superintendent adds governance to his or her CEO leadership portfolio, putting it high on the list of critical executive functions. This means that the superintendent devotes the time required to become a true expert in this complex, rapidly changing field and that he or she regularly dedicates a large chunk of time—somewhere in the range of 20 to 25 percent—to thinking about the governance function and working directly with the board. Making the board a top CEO priority means not sitting back and waiting for the board to develop itself as a governing body. Rather, he or she assumes primary responsibility for helping the board to develop its "governing design" in the interest of higher-impact governing: defining its role, mapping out its governing work, and developing the structure and processes to accomplish this work. The board-savvy superintendent is a board capacity builder par excellence.

- **Consciously Focuses on the Human Dimension of the Board-Superintendent Partnership**
  The board-savvy superintendent views his or her partnership with the board as a precious and fragile bond that can be easily broken if not conscientiously and continuously maintained. One of the most important ways of maintaining the board–superintendent partnership is to consciously manage the human dimension of the relationship, paying close attention to the psychological "care and feeding" of board members, focusing on meeting their ego needs, and employing strategies to build feelings of ownership and commitment among them. Another way is to ensure effective two-way communication. A well-designed process for regular board evaluation of CEO performance can also be a powerful vehicle for keeping the board–CEO partnership healthy.

- **Functions as a Full-Fledged, Contemporary CEO**
  Board-savvy superintendents do not see themselves narrowly as chief administrative officers whose primary responsibility is representing the

administrative staff to the board. Rather, they know that they are full-fledged CEOs, and as more leaders than administrators, they consequently study CEOship, acquiring the knowledge and skills of contemporary CEOs.

BRINGING THE RIGHT ATTITUDE

If you bring a control-bias or a negative, defensive attitude to your work with your board, you are highly likely to end up with an underperforming board and a poor working board–superintendent relationship. The board-savvy superintendent looks at the board and sees a precious asset, not a damage-control challenge, and views one of his or her most important responsibilities as ensuring that the board's tremendous leadership potential is fully realized in practice. The board-savvy superintendent also sees the board as his or her preeminent partner in leading the school district, and accordingly devotes close attention to building the partnership and keeping it healthy. This makes the best of sense for three key reasons. First, your board is truly a precious resource, in terms of accumulated experience, diverse expertise, community influence, and networks of associations. Second, you need the best thinking of your board in fashioning strategies to address complex issues facing your district. Third, if you allow a gap to persist between the leadership potential of the high-achieving, demanding people on your board and actual governing practice, you will reap a whirlwind of frustration, irritation, eventually anger, and often the total disintegration of your working partnership with the board.

AVOIDING A DANGEROUS VACUUM

This view of the board as a precious asset and rich resource for decision making flies in the face of the traditional control bias of CEOs when dealing with their boards. Involving your board more creatively and proactively in district affairs can feel like opening the proverbial Pandora's box, putting you and your executives at risk. We believe, based on long experience, that when boards behave dysfunctionally—and they sometimes do, of course!—making foolish decisions or meddling in administrative matters, it is seldom because of malevolence. Indeed, the overwhelming majority of school board members we have encountered over the years, including resident curmudgeons who can be taxing partners, sincerely do want to do a good job of governing. They believe in high-quality education and are dedicated to community service. Of course, now and then you will encounter a truly "bad apple"—the person who comes on the board with a gigantic ax to grind and cares not a whit about the broader governing responsibilities of the board. Fortunately, in our experience, these incorrigible board members are a rarity, and tend to alienate their board colleagues very quickly, thus limiting the damage they can cause.

The problem in virtually every situation we have witnessed is a vacuum in board governing design, which leaves the board at sea in terms of its governing role, work, and processes. In a vacuum, high-achieving type A personalities will find something to do that makes them feel productive, and if they do not know how to produce high-impact governance, then they will gravitate to lower-impact governance. Whether you like it or not, they *will* keep busy, and so your challenge is to take the bull by the horns, helping them to move to high-impact performance, even if at first it feels dangerous to you. If you give in to the need for control, you cannot play a creative role in building an enduring, close partnership with your board.

MAKING GOVERNANCE A TOP PRIORITY

Putting governance on your short list of top priorities means that your board is always a giant blip on your CEO radar screen. It means that you allocate significant time and detailed attention to board affairs, that you become a true expert in this complex, evolving field, and that you make a strong commitment to board capacity building. Experience has taught us that somewhere in the range of 20 to 25 percent of a CEO's time on the average should be devoted to thinking about, developing, supporting, and interacting with the board. If the time allocation falls much below 20 percent for very long, you can expect trouble to appear in the form of board underperformance and dysfunction in the board–CEO partnership. We are talking about quality time, not merely schmoozing over breakfasts and lunches with particular board members. Serious reading about the field of governance and fashioning strategies for board capacity building are examples of higher use of your precious time.

Since governance is a relatively new field in terms of serious attention, governance literature is filled with conventional wisdom and the field is rapidly developing, your becoming an expert on governing boards is a real challenge. One thing for sure: you must go beyond the boundaries of educational administration in educating yourself on governance. One inexpensive, time-efficient approach is to build a library of periodicals and books on governance. We recommend that you take a look at publications dealing with for-profit governance as well as those focusing on the nonprofit and public sectors. One of the richest sources of information is the BoardSource (formerly the National Center for Nonprofit Boards), which has commissioned the publication of a whole library of relatively brief, very practical monographs on virtually every facet of governing board operations. The National School Boards Association (NSBA) is another major source, and other national associations such as the American Association of School Administrators (AASA) are beginning to pay more attention to governance in their publications and educational programs.

You can also learn about the work of governing by serving on national, state, and local boards yourself, bringing the lessons you learn back to your own boardroom. At the very least, you will gain a better understanding of the intricacies of governing and the informational and other needs of board members. Even if you spend some time on a dysfunctional underperforming board you can learn valuable lessons about what does not work in the governing arena. Diverse board service will also introduce you to various styles of CEO leadership, giving you a better understanding of your own CEO functions as they relate to governance.

Making governance one of your top CEO priorities also means that you take accountability for helping your board to strengthen its governing capacity, which we discuss in detail in chapter 2. Board-savvy superintendents aggressively promote and support board capacity building, primarily by engaging their boards in the creative and demanding process of rethinking what we call their "governing design": the board's role, its work, and the processes and structure that it employs in carrying out its governing work. You cannot realistically sit back and expect your board to take the initiative in its own capacity building. As part-time volunteers who are typically under considerable pressure, they are likely not even to see the need for capacity building; indeed, they might not even be aware that higher impact governance is an option, much less a need. As part-timers in the field of educational governance, they cannot be expected to become experts in the field; that is your responsibility as CEO. Therefore, if you are truly committed to high-impact governance and to a close, productive working partnership with your board, you have no choice but to become a persistent, thoughtful board capacity builder, getting your board interested in, and committed to, capacity building and helping them go through the process of updating their governing design.

MANAGING THE HUMAN DIMENSION OF THE PARTNERSHIP

You can be a superstar at board capacity building, superbly handling the process of updating the board's governing design, and still fail at managing the more human dimension of the partnership. CEOship is also often described as in large measure the "business" of building and maintaining close, productive, harmonious relationships with key constituents inside and outside an organization, including the board, executive team, and faculty in a school system. School boards are, of course, above all else people—not *just* people, but typically high-achieving, experienced, influential, and occasionally demanding and impatient people. The people populating school boards are likely to be difficult to work with, and so the board-savvy superintendent must be a highly accomplished relationship manager.

This means cultivating a deep understanding of the principles that underlie successful working relationships and systematically applying this knowledge in your day-to-day work with your board. For example, it is widely recognized that the feeling of ownership is a powerful generator of feelings of commitment and satisfaction, for human beings generally and definitely for boards. Experience has taught us that feeling like an owner of something depends on playing a meaningful role in generating or shaping that thing. Take the annual budget as an example. No one would recommend that your school board get involved in detail in developing your district's annual budget, but if you merely develop the budget document, send it in finished form to your board, and expect them to feel ownership from thumbing through it and asking questions, guess again.

Board-savvy superintendents with whom we are familiar have dealt with this issue successfully by first making sure that a committee of the board is accountable for the board's participation in budget development, and, second, by finding "levers" that the board can pull without meddling in inappropriate detail. For example, one superintendent who was a virtuoso at relationship management helped her board's planning committee chair a pre-budget operational planning session early in the budget preparation process, at which each associate superintendent presented an assessment of environmental changes in her or his field, identified critical issues emerging from the assessment, discussed operational innovation targets being contemplated to address the issues, and uncovered the cost parameters of tackling these targets. This prefinancial dialogue enabled board members to offer input that the superintendent and her associate superintendents could take into consideration in fashioning their detailed plans and budgets. For example, an athletic director was told to bring back concrete strategies for beefing up security at football games after a discussion of the accelerating violence over the past couple of years.

Communication is a glue that helps to cement a strong board–superintendent working relationship, provided that it is pertinent, honest, and accurate in content, that it is provided in a timely fashion, and that it is formatted for ease of understanding. First and foremost, of course, your board needs information to carry out its core governing functions; for example, your board's performance oversight committee should regularly see reports on educational and financial performance that enable the committee to assess district effectiveness and efficiency in carrying out its educational mission. At a more personal level, your board requires regular communication aimed at strengthening its capacity as a governing body, providing insights about the board–CEO partnership, and preserving its public credibility and reputation.

Therefore, board-savvy superintendents keep their boards well briefed on major developments in the fields of K–12 education and governance, and they take the trouble to keep their boards apprised of their individual CEO activities, above and beyond the overall educational activities of the district.

For example, they brief their boards on their work on other boards, on their involvement in state and national association work, on their speaking engagements, and the like. They also make sure that board members are never unpleasantly surprised by major events in the environment that leave them looking uninformed and inept. Nothing can unglue a partnership faster than one of the partners looking foolish because of the other partner's failure to communicate important information.

In chapter 4 we take a detailed look at board evaluation of the CEO as one of the single most powerful ways to keep the board–superintendent working partnership close and healthy. Suffice it to say at this point that board-savvy superintendents make sure that the board regularly, thoroughly evaluates their performance, employing a well-designed process that is CEO-specific and focuses on outcomes, not merely functional excellence as measured by a checklist questionnaire of some kind. A well-designed and executed evaluation process can ensure that the board and superintendent are in detailed agreement on CEO performance expectations and on the areas where CEO performance needs to be strengthened.

FUNCTIONING AS A FULL-FLEDGED CEO

The title "superintendent" is somewhat anachronistic and misleading, harking back to bygone years when the top job in school districts was seen largely in operational and administrative terms. Superintending an institution—whether a school district, prison, or water purification plant—essentially meant keeping it running efficiently (and perhaps most important, keeping the inmates, or students, under control). In the traditional view, the school district superintendent's role was confined to hands-on direction and oversight of the educational, administrative, and operational functions of the school system, while the board's was to set broad directions and to fashion policies to govern operations. Applying this narrow conception of your role as a superintendent would, as you surely know, be a recipe for failure in working with your board in today's world.

The superintendents who in our experience are most effective at working with their school boards—who build close, enduring partnerships that really *do* generate high-impact governance—function as full-fledged, contemporary

CEOs, seeing themselves more fully as *leaders*, not just chief administrators. They embrace CEOship broadly as their preeminent field, transcending educational administration, now that they sit in the superintendent's seat. In practical terms, this means that they strive to become knowledgeable—indeed, to become experts—in the complex, ever-changing field of CEOship (within the wider field of leadership). These modern superintendent/leaders broaden their reading beyond the confines of educational administration to include CEOship generally, for example, by seeking out journals that excel in teaching leadership and CEOship, such as the *Harvard Business Review*, and books that analyze leadership and profile leaders, including biographies. They also become acute observers of CEOs in action, looking for both models and, closer at hand, mentors who can teach CEOship in practical terms.

As we mentioned in the preface, you need to keep in mind as you explore the various dimensions of CEOship that as a superintendent you are more constrained in carrying out your CEO role than the CEOs of most for-profit corporations. Your discretion as CEO is limited by state legislation and regulations, and your board will expect a far higher degree of involvement in district affairs than the board of the typical for-profit corporation. Your job is much more public than a corporate CEO's and is the subject of much more intense scrutiny. And, of course, the basic "production process" of a school district—what happens in the classroom—is far less amenable to your influence than the process that a for-profit corporation employs. Even with these in-built constraints, however, you are still well advised to think of yourself as a full-fledged CEO rather than as merely the most senior administrator in your district.

UNLEARNING AS A DEVELOPMENTAL TOOL

In mastering the field of contemporary CEOship, unlearning can be just as important to you as acquiring new knowledge and functions. Working with hundreds of CEOs over the years, including many school district superintendents, we have learned that the very attributes, skills, and work habits that can help you climb the educational career ladder—for many, from classroom teacher through unit leader, department head, principal, associate superintendent— can become hindrances once you have reached the top spot in your district. Ironically, excellent classroom teaching may be better preparation for contemporary CEOship than traditional educational administration, since effective teachers pay close attention to clearly communicating often-complex ideas and to actively facilitating (rather than focusing on controlling) discussion. But once you have ventured into the terrain of educational administration, producing finished staff work based on meticulous logic and good information and expeditiously coming up with "right" answers become prized qualities that can work against you as a superintendent dealing with your school board.

Also, of course, some of the most important functions of CEOs, including superintendents of schools, cannot easily be learned by climbing the career ladder. For example, you might have little—or only formal—interaction with the school board before you become your district's CEO, meaning that you are faced with having to do some high-stakes catch-up in the field of governance. Or you might never have played a leading role in strategic decision making, which is one of the most important functions of a high-impact governing board. The combination of administrative skills that need to be unlearned with the lack of expertise in critical areas can be deadly, professionally speaking, unless you bring the right instincts to the job (for example, understanding the importance of building feelings of ownership among board members) and are blessed with a period of relative calm and stability during which you can learn the job. No one ever said that CEOship should be easy!

BEYOND ADMINISTRATION

The contemporary superintendent/leader is not constrained by an artificial distinction between "administration"—the preserve of the superintendent—and "policy"—the board's terrain. These board-savvy superintendent/leaders do not see themselves narrowly as chief administrative officers of their school districts, who are a distinctly different breed from their boards. They do not cultivate a distant, hands-off role vis-à-vis the governance function. Rather, they take a fuller view of their CEO leadership role, seeing themselves as full partners with their boards, who are active collaborators and participants in the work of governing and aggressive builders of their boards' governing capacity.

Indeed, the contemporary superintendent/CEO sees the top job in the school district as a unique hybrid position—a blend of board member and chief administrator, neither exclusively one nor the other. As you know, this more nuanced view of CEOship has long been predominant in the for-profit sector, where a corporate CEO always sits on his or her board of directors, and frequently even chairs the board. In the nonprofit sector, while a CEO would never chair the board, it is becoming more common to see the CEO as a nonvoting or full-fledged member of the board. We do not recommend that superintendents sit on their boards (although we do not oppose the idea), but we strongly recommend moving beyond the we–they dynamic that is still common in board–superintendent relations.

MORE THAN COMMANDER-IN-CHIEF

Leadership—the somewhat amorphous field that, as a modern superintendent/CEO, you share with your school board—encompasses a variety of knowledge, skills, and executive functions. If you aspire to lead your school district as a contemporary, full-fledged CEO, you need to move beyond the simplistic but still widely popular conception of the leader as a commander-in-chief. To be sure, having a commanding presence, being able to articulate a vision and to employ inspiring rhetoric *are* important leadership traits, particularly in times of crisis, and such popular, calcium-laden phrases as "the buck stops here" and "it happens on my watch" do capture a dimension of leadership (and hence of CEOship). But if you aspire to be a board-savvy superintendent, you must master less dramatic, technically more subtle leadership functions that have to do with building the capacity of your board to provide high-impact governance. Among the most important if you aspire to be board-savvy are (1) honing your skills in organizational architecture/design and facilitation, and (2) becoming an expert in the field of strategic planning and decision making, which is without question the gold standard for high-impact governing boards.

Architect/Designer

Chief executives are often described these days as preeminently organizational architects and designers, meaning that they devote significant time and thought to developing and fitting together the major components of the organization they are accountable for leading: the structures, systems, and processes that make it possible to perform the functions required to carry out the organization's mission successfully. For example, the board-savvy superintendent pays close attention to the *design* of the school board as an organization: its mission, its governing work, and the structure (e.g., committees) and processes it employs in doing its governing work.

But the board, in carrying out its governing functions, must draw on and interface with other school district systems and processes, such as strategic planning, annual operational planning and budget preparation, and information management. If the connections are not carefully made (for example, exactly how the board and perhaps one of its committees will participate in the development of the annual budget), then the school board's decision-making impact will be reduced and its satisfaction eroded.

Facilitation

In our experience, CEOs who build strong, positive, enduring partnerships with their boards are inevitably highly skilled facilitators of process, basically because board involvement in helping to generate important outcomes, as we noted earlier, is the only reliable way to turn your board into owners who are strongly committed. Successful facilitation of process involves, first, designing the process to be facilitated (for example, an annual board–superintendent–executive team strategic planning retreat) and, second, helping people to go through the process successfully. Facilitation more often than not entails leading "from behind," helping people to discover their own answers through their participation in well-designed process. For example, you might employ breakout groups in a retreat to identify and flesh out first-cut strategic issues facing your school district.

Facilitation is the polar opposite of either training your board in how to behave or to accomplish its governing work or sending your board a document with the "right" answers. Neither of these traditional approaches is likely to generate ownership or commitment among your board members. One of your challenges as CEO of your district will be to resist the simple, traditional approach of sending your board final answers to really strategic questions that are complex, involve high stakes, and require strong board commitment that is likely to be tested during implementation. The Morningside Heights school closing vignette we presented earlier in this chapter is a classic how-not-to case of failing to design and facilitate a high-stakes process. There will be instances, by the way, where it will make sense for you as your district's CEO to secure the services of a professional facilitator from outside the district to lead your board through a process where your facilitation might be suspect (for example, in working through the division of labor between the CEO and the board), but the principle of employing facilitation to achieve firm commitment does not change.

Strategic Decision Making

Strategic planning and decision making would make the top of any list for creative and proactive board involvement in generating high-impact governance in your school district. In fact, this critical function is so important that it is widely considered the gold standard for board involvement in leadership, and we devote chapter 3 to your working with your board in making strategic decisions aimed at producing significant innovation in your district. In light of the importance of this function to high-impact governance, being board-savvy means that you will become an expert in strategic planning and decision making, understanding the significant developments in the field, and—wearing your architect/designer hat—making sure that these developments are factored into the design of your district's strategic planning process and of your board's involvement in it.

Perhaps the most dramatic change in the field, which we discuss in detail in chapter 3, is the demise of traditional, comprehensive long-range planning for arbitrary and largely meaningless periods such as five or ten years. Replacing this cumbersome, document-fixated process is a more much focused approach that homes in on particular strategic issues facing an organization, fashioning strategic change initiatives to address these issues, and meticulously managing the implementation of these initiatives. You will want to make sure that you understand these startling developments in the field of planning, and that your district's planning process incorporates them; otherwise, you put yourself at risk as the CEO of losing credibility and board support because of disappointing planning outcomes. The least-savvy thing that you could possibly do is merely to "buy" a consultant's canned, outdated approach on the basis of your lack of knowledge.

UPDATING YOUR BOARD'S GOVERNING DESIGN

A CLEAR CHOICE

After going back to basics, briefly examining different ways of seeing non profit and public governing boards, we concentrate in chapter 2 on the development of your board as an organizational entity, which involves fashioning and periodically updating your board's governing design. Every board in existence has a clear choice: merely inherit the board of the past or consciously and systematically design the board that your district's strategic leadership team—board, superintendent, and executive staff—want now and in the future. Inheritance, unfortunately, continues to be a popular choice, but serious attention to board organizational design is the surest path to high-impact governance, and making sure that it is done well is one of your most important responsibilities as superintendent.

Our aim in chapter 2 is to provide you with detailed, practical, well-tested guidance that you can apply in carrying out this board organizational design responsibility. We discuss ways that you can convince your board members to participate in updating the board's governing design, and we describe how you can employ an intensive work session, or retreat, to get the design process well on the road. We then examine each of the key steps in the governing design process, which involves developing (1) the people on your board, (2) your board's governing mission and detailed governing work, and (3) your board's structure.

A FRESH LOOK AT BOARDS

As we were putting together our first-cut outline of *The Board-Savvy Superintendent* in fall 2001, we asked ourselves two fundamental questions: first, what is a governing board, and second, what is the work of governing? You might be tempted to respond to the first question dismissively; after all, the answer might seem pretty obvious: A board is an organization's policy-making body. We realized, as we thought about the question, that this is too simple a description of the board. In reality, boards are highly complex organizational entities that can be seen in three very positive ways: (1) as a precious asset on which your school district can capitalize, (2) as a vehicle for community leaders to volunteer in a very special and demanding way—governing the affairs of your school district, and (3) as an organizational entity within your wider school district organization that can be developed along various lines in order to produce stronger governing performance.

A PRECIOUS ASSET

Boards are without question one of your school district's most precious assets, as we discussed in chapter 1. Board members bring to your district's boardroom wide-ranging professional and personal experience, varied knowledge and expertise, diverse perspectives on complex issues, visibility and clout in the community, and networks of associations with key school district stakeholders, such as city hall, the chamber of commerce, and various civic organizations. Unfortunately, however, boards—including many school boards—are almost certainly among our nation's most underexploited precious assets, as evidenced by the quite common and startlingly large gap between the tremendous leadership promise of the average board and its real-life governing performance. We strongly believe that one of your most important responsibilities as a board-savvy superintendent is to ensure that your school district realizes the full benefits of capitalizing to the maximum on this rich asset.

A VEHICLE FOR VOLUNTEERING

Volunteering to advance the public good is one of America's noblest traditions, now being exported throughout the world. In no other country in human history have great fortunes been given away so enthusiastically with fewer strings attached; nowhere else in the world have so many people volunteered their time to such a wide array of nonprofit and public institutions and organizations. Public and nonprofit boards of all shapes and sizes, including school boards, provide millions of Americans with an opportunity to volunteer in a very special and complex way: to govern the affairs of an organization.

Later in this chapter, we take a detailed look at what makes up your school board's governing work. For now, keep in mind that governing a school district basically means making judgments and decisions that, on a continuing basis, determine where our district is headed over the long run, what our district essentially is right now, and how well our district is performing—educationally, administratively, and financially. School boards, like all other boards we have worked with, do other, nongoverning work, which can make a valuable contribution to the welfare of your district: for example, speaking on behalf of your district during a tax levy campaign or sitting on the dais at graduation. The challenge is to make sure the essential governing is done in a full and timely fashion, without letting the nongoverning work claim more than its fair share of your board members' time and energy.

AN ORGANIZATION

We pointed out in chapter 1 that, by definition, your school board is an organization, a formally constituted, permanent entity in your school district, consisting of people working together through formal structure and process to achieve a common mission: to govern. Your first impulse might be to say, "Ho hum, so what, but thanks for sharing that with me." However, keep in mind that, because your school board is an organization like any other unit in your school district, whether the department of curriculum and instruction, the office of the superintendent, or a particular middle school, it can be consciously developed as an organization to make it more effective and efficient. It stands to reason that if a school board and its superintendent work closely together in developing the board as an organization, that board, like any other organizational unit in the world, is likely to perform its governing work more effectively and efficiently.

THE BOARD GOVERNING DESIGN

The acid test of whether you are truly a board-savvy superintendent is that your board really does function as what we call a high-impact governing body. In our experience, high-impact governing boards above all else concentrate on carrying out their governing work fully, regularly answering the three fundamental questions about where our school district is going, what it is right now, and how it is performing. In order to build the capacity to provide high-impact governance, these boards engage in formal, systematic board organizational development, fashioning and periodically updating as appropriate what we call the board governing design, consisting of three key elements:

- The conscious, systematic development of the board as a human resource, not only influencing the election or appointment of board members, but also ensuring that their governing skills are systematically developed;
- The detailed mapping out of the board's governing work, beginning with the development of a high-level board governing mission to serve as a framework for the more detailed definition of the ongoing decisions and judgments that the board makes in governing a school district;
- And the design of a committee structure that will support and facilitate the board's accomplishing its governing work.

One of the great ironies in the governance "business," is that—while boards are widely described as the preeminent policy-making body in any organization—many if not most boards and their CEOs, in our experience, devote little if any serious time to systematic board organizational development. They go about their governing work, in other words, without having thought through their governing design. If we ran our schools like we run many if not most school boards, our communities would be in an uproar. However, people tend not to set high standards for board governing performance, and as a consequence are not upset by lackluster governance. We reject these low governing standards, and we passionately believe that you, as your district's CEO, are accountable for seeing that your school board is systematically developed as an organization and is guided by a clear, detailed governing design that ensures high-impact governance.

GETTING YOUR BOARD ON THE DESIGN TRACK

In an ideal world, the members of your school board would jump at the chance to further develop the board as an organization in the interest of strengthening its governing performance. Ideally, they would see the gap between the board's leadership potential and current performance. After all, your board members are bright, energetic, committed citizens who sincerely want to provide strong leadership for the district. However, in the real world, as experience has taught us, you should set off on the board organizational development journey keenly aware of the significant barriers you are likely to encounter in getting your board's commitment to participate in updating its governing design. For one thing, the governing "train" is already running, keeping your board members quite busy as it is, and the prospect of putting on the brakes long enough to rethink what kind of governing work the board should be doing and how the board might be better structured may not be immediately appealing to many, if any, of your board members. And if already-busy board members think that the design activity might increase the time they must devote to governing, then the initial resistance is likely to be even higher.

You should also keep in mind that many if not most of your board members might be quite content with the board's governing performance now because, not having a clear picture of the governing outcomes that a strong board can generate, they do not see a governing performance gap to be filled. And there is always the quite normal human resistance to any change at all that typically comes from two sources. One is fear of failing to perform well at doing something new; we have never met a high-achieving person who relished the prospect of appearing inept in public. The specter of embarrassment surely strikes greater terror in the hearts of high-achieving type A personalities than the more abstract threat of death. The other source of resistance is comfort with things the way they are. Many board members we have met over the years have, through ambition, tenacity, and sometimes high tolerance for pain, "learned the ropes" on boards well enough to exert significant influence in the governing process. To them, if only unconsciously, it might not be a perfect board, but they have learned to make it work for them, and they are not about to have it tampered with.

There are some tried-and-true ways that you can employ to stimulate your board members' appetite for participating in updating the board's governing design. However, attempting to directly convince the board as a whole—sitting together in plenary session—to step back from the fray and participate in rethinking its governing role, processes, and structure is unlikely to succeed. You can try the course of directly preaching to and teaching your board as a whole, but board members tend to be impervious to direct lobbying from their CEOs, primarily because CEOs are commonly perceived as too interested in advancing their own positions vis-à-vis their boards to be completely trusted.

ENLISTING DESIGN CHAMPIONS

Since your direct lobbying to the board as a whole is likely to meet a brick wall, we suggest that your first step be to develop what we call design champions on the board who will promote the design process to their board colleagues. The ideal place to start is your current board president or chair, then enlist his or her help in recruiting two or three other board colleagues, perhaps the members of the board's executive committee, if your board has one, or the chairs of your board's standing committees, if any. Turning selected board members into governing design champions can be accomplished by raising their sights in terms of the board's leadership potential, educating them on the key features of high-impact governance, convincing them that enough of a governing performance gap exists to justify rethinking the board's governing design, and acquainting them with the process required to update the design.

Board-savvy CEOs, including several superintendents whom we have observed over the years, have employed a number of techniques for educating potential board design champions on high-impact governance as a way of whetting their appetites for the governing design process. One of the easiest and least expensive is to share pertinent publications on governance. Although busy board members might not have time to read a book, they will almost always be willing to look at an article. You might try your hand at summarizing one or more pertinent articles in a memorandum that is tailored to your audience, translating ideas into language you know will communicate effectively.

A more elaborate and expensive approach, but one that we have seen work very well, is for the superintendent to arrange for the board president/chair, and perhaps one or more other board members, to attend a workshop on governance. Increasing numbers of colleges and universities are offering programs on nonprofit and public governance, national associations such as the American Association of School Administrators—along with its state affiliates—and the National School Boards Association offer sessions on board leadership at their annual and other meetings, and BoardSource (formerly the National Center for Nonprofit Boards) provides a number of educational programs throughout the year.

Educating your potential board design champions on high-impact governance and appealing to their altruism are, alone, unlikely to secure their firm commitment to take the lead in getting your board to participate in updating its governing design. Experience has taught us that you will be well advised to tap into a more selfish vein. We have seen several superintendents who have solidified the commitment of board design champions by focusing on the satisfaction that higher-impact governance can provide them (along the lines of "Life is short, you've devoted precious time and energy in abundance to the board, you shouldn't settle for anything less than a truly satisfying experience in return for all your effort, so go for the gusto!"). A highly effective technique is to appeal to board members' very natural desire to have an enduring impact, to leave an indelible imprint. One superintendent successfully signed on her board chair as the leading design champion by drumming in the concept of "your leaving a legacy" in the form of more effective board leadership.

ONCE YOU HAVE DESIGN CHAMPIONS ON BOARD

The point of convincing your board chair and perhaps other board members to serve as design champions is to secure the board's commitment to participate in updating its governing design. We have found that two approaches have worked very well in translating this commitment into practice. One is for the board president or chair to appoint an ad hoc governance task force to review developments in the field of public and nonprofit governance, to assess the current governing practices of the school board, and to recommend initiatives aimed at strengthening the board's governing work, structure, and processes. Another approach that we have found to be a more effective vehicle for moving the board organizational design process forward is for the board president, perhaps with the concurrence of the board's executive committee, to call for a special board work session—popularly known as a retreat—for the purpose of kicking off the governing design process and producing a rough-cut version of the governing design that can be fleshed out later.

One thing is for sure: you and your school board are well advised not to attempt to handle board organizational design through your board's regular business meeting. Sustained time and attention away from a business-as-usual setting are essential for raising board members' sights above the operational details that clutter the normal board agenda. Even if you go the ad hoc task force route rather than holding a design retreat, you will want to review the task force's report in one or more intensive board work sessions separate from the regular business meeting.

Retreats are extremely powerful vehicles for taking school boards a good distance along the road of board organizational development if they are meticulously designed and conducted. What they do very effectively is to educate board members and to build their feelings of ownership and commitment through the process of discovery, rather than by teaching, preaching, and exhorting. Board governing design retreats, in our experience, are likely to be successful when (1) at least a full day is set aside for the retreat; (2) board members are involved in designing the retreat; (3) a professional facilitator is retained to assist in designing, facilitating, and following up on the retreat; (4) a detailed retreat design is developed in advance, including the process for following through on the retreat; (5) the retreat is highly participatory and involves board members in leading deliberations; (6) the superintendent and his or her executive team are full participants along with the board; and (7) no final decisions are made in the retreat.

Keep in mind that a full-fledged, day-long, facilitated retreat dedicated to board organizational development is not likely to be required every year. However, if your board has not within the past three years taken a day away from the boardroom to rethink its governing role, work, and structure, or if your board is exhibiting symptoms of serious dysfunction (such as frequent angry outbursts at meetings or constantly being bogged down in minutiae), your board is a prime candidate for the retreat approach. In our experience, many school boards—having gone through an intensive governing design retreat—can make do for the next two or three years with half-day board tune-up work sessions, often as part of an annual strategic planning retreat focusing on strategic issues and major innovation initiatives (see chapter 3 for a detailed description of such a strategic planning event).

ENSURING A SUCCESSFUL RETREAT

One way of involving board members in planning a governing design retreat is for your board president/chair to appoint three or four board members to serve as an ad hoc retreat design committee, which is responsible for developing the detailed design of the retreat.

Of course, the participation of board members in planning their own work session is a sure-fire way of turning them into owners of the event—second-stage design champions, if you will. Retaining an independent professional facilitator to work with the ad hoc retreat design committee, to facilitate the retreat, and to play a role in following through on the retreat is one of the more important ways of ensuring that the retreat will be productive and ultimately produce a powerful return on your district's investment of time and money in the event. We strongly recommend that if your ad hoc retreat design committee decides to retain a professional facilitator, it screens potential facilitators carefully, making sure that they bring not only extensive successful experience in running similar sessions, but also in-depth knowledge in the field of nonprofit and public governance.

A fully developed retreat design will include the following components: the objectives that the retreat is intended to achieve (e.g., to clarify our board's governing mission, to map out our board's governing role and work in detail, to strengthen our board's committee structure), the structure of the retreat (e.g., the location, the use of breakout groups to generate specific outcomes, such as a profile of desirable board members' attributes and qualifications), and the blow-by-blow agenda. Breakout groups can be an effective way to ensure active participation if their outcomes and methodology are clearly specified in the retreat design, and using board members as breakout group leaders is a reliable way of providing them with ego satisfaction and strengthening their ownership of the retreat results. We strongly recommend, by the way, that not only the superintendent participate in the retreat, but also all of the superintendent's senior administrators—the executive team—for three important reasons: to educate executive team members on governance generally and on the expectations and needs of their board particularly, to build board–executive teamwork, and to ensure follow-through on the retreat.

Experience in conducting board organizational design retreats has taught us that you will be wise to avoid attempting to reach formal consensus or to make final decisions during only a day or so together, for two major reasons. First, forcing people to arrive at firm conclusions in such a short time is highly likely to increase the tension in the room, to stymie discussion, and to decrease enjoyment. More important, "seat-of-the-pants" decision making—although it might appeal to the type A desire to tie all loose ends neatly—is likely to produce decisions that are half-baked and last not much longer than the following Monday. A thorough follow-through process can ensure that the results of an open brainstorming process are analyzed and that decisions are eventually made and implemented.

For example, let's say that one of the products generated by a breakout group during the retreat is a rough-cut governing mission. Follow-up might include (1) the facilitator's cleaning up and refining the mission statement as part of her follow-up action report on the retreat, (2) the ad hoc retreat design committee's reviewing the facilitator's report line by line and further refining the governing mission, and (3) the full board's eventually adopting the governing mission by formal resolution. Combining free-flowing brainstorming with a rigorous follow-through process ultimately saves time that might otherwise be spent going back to the drawing boards because of half-baked decisions, while ensuring that the final retreat product reflects retreat participants' open, creative deliberations. You should always keep in mind that the premature application of discipline (such as having to formally rank-order the elements of a profile of desirable board member attributes) only provides the illusion of precision, while squelching discussion and prematurely narrowing perspectives.

BOARD HUMAN RESOURCE DEVELOPMENT

Boards are essentially people, and the quality of your board's governance is heavily dependent on the cast of characters on your school board—on the attributes and qualifications that they bring with them to the boardroom, on their commitment to governance, on their knowledge and skills in the field of governance, and on their performance against well-defined standards and targets. No matter how well crafted your board's governing mission, how clearly defined your board's role and governing work, or how effective your board's committee structure, your board cannot become a truly high-impact governing body without paying serious attention to its development as a human resource.

We know what you are likely to be saying to yourself at this point: "Wait a minute! You're venturing into la-la land now. As a superintendent, I don't have any influence on the makeup of my board, which is elected, and if I did get involved in trying to affect who gets elected I'd be in a heap of trouble pretty fast." You would certainly be right about avoiding direct political action; if you did become involved in school board election campaigns, you would want to update your curriculum vitae and keep your eye on professional opportunities elsewhere. Even if your school board is appointed by a third party, say, the mayor, you would be well advised to be very careful about offering your advice and counsel on filling vacancies on your board. Being perceived as politically neutral is without question an asset for a CEO in the public and nonprofit sector.

What we do want you to know, however, is that you can assist your board in developing itself as a human resource without putting yourself at risk professionally; indeed, you are obligated to do so, in light of the stakes involved. This is a classic situation calling for your facilitation skills and requiring that you lead from behind, helping your board to do what it needs to be doing without appearing to be the prime mover. Your challenge is to convince your board to begin to manage itself as a human resource, within whatever "constitutional" boundaries have been established (e.g., an appointed or elected school board) and current political realities (e.g., a mayor who definitely does not welcome advice and counsel on appointments). Five steps have proved to be very effective in developing the people on school boards:

- Give serious thought to the desirable board composition.
- Employ this thinking in some appropriate, realistic way in influencing the process of filling board vacancies.
- Annually adopt a formal, detailed, annual board governing–skills development program and budget.
- Set governing performance targets for the board as a whole and for its members individually.
- Assign responsibility for board human resource development to a particular standing committee of the board.

Board Composition

Thinking about the desired composition of your school board is a matter of considering the broad mix of people on your school board in terms of such categories as gender, race, constituency affiliations, occupation, and the like, and also considering individual member traits and qualifications that are likely to contribute to high-impact governance. Individual attributes and qualifications tend to remain relatively constant, although over time the profile of the desirable board member can be elaborated and refined, based on experience. The desired mix of board members, by contrast, tends to be more situational. For example, we have worked with school boards that clearly saw the need to diversify the mix of people on the board to accomplish critical aims, for example, to increase high-level business representation in order to strengthen business community understanding and support, especially during the tax levy campaign anticipated the year after next, and to increase minority representation to reflect the changing demographics of the district.

If your board has not paid much attention to developing its composition in the recent past, then it makes sense to deal with this facet of board organizational development at a day-long retreat. Thereafter, at least for three or four years, updating the desired board composition might be handled by the board committee that is responsible for board human resource development. Many boards that we have worked with have at such a retreat employed a breakout group to identify a desirable mix of board members and to fashion a preliminary profile of desired board member attributes and qualifications, which was subsequently refined and finalized by one of the board's standing committees. One board, for example, fashioned a profile consisting of a number of elements that completed the sentence, "We need members on our board who. . . ." Among the elements were "are strongly committed to high-quality public education"; "are able and willing to commit the time necessary to govern our district effectively"; "believe in strong board leadership and are willing to sharpen their governing skills"; "have acquired governing experience through successful service on other boards"; and "are team players, committed to active collaboration with their board colleagues."

Getting People onto the Board

What makes such a board composition exercise worth the time is follow-through, of course. Even when, as is the case with virtually all public school boards, a board is not self-appointing (as many nonprofit boards are), it is feasible and highly recommended to put such thinking to good use, albeit indirectly. For example, if your school board members are elected, it makes the best of sense to circulate your board member profile of desired attributes and qualifications widely in the community, perhaps paying special attention to getting the word out to civic organizations. If one or more citizens' groups in your community plays an active role in getting qualified candidates to run for the school board, then these groups would be prime targets. And even if your board is appointed by a chief elected official in your community, the board can always make sure that he or she receives the profile.

Your board can put the profile to good use in other ways. For example, some school boards have incorporated their profile into a comprehensive orientation manual for new board members. Others have employed the profile as a device to pique the interest of community residents who might otherwise not have thought about contending for a seat on the board. Keep in mind that the profile can also be a means for building the school board's reputation and credibility in your community—as evidence of the board's commitment to high-performance governance.

Such credibility building can obviously strengthen the board's case for continued and expanded community financial support for the schools, as well as attracting the business sector's support and collaboration and even making the board more of a magnet for attracting talented people to board service. Finally, devoting time and effort to fashioning and periodically updating the profile tends to solemnize the work of governing among board members themselves, strengthening their "governing self-esteem," inspiring them to greater effort in governing, and melding them into a more effective governing team.

Many board-savvy superintendents we have known have encouraged their boards to make systematic use of citizen advisory committees and task forces, which can serve as a kind of board "farm system." These superintendents pay close attention to such volunteers, constantly on the lookout for potential school board members who can be encouraged to run for board seats or brought to the attention of appointing authorities.

Governing Skills Development

Although making a continuous effort to strengthen the composition of your school board is an important avenue to higher-impact governance, we have learned through experience that virtually anyone who is suitably motivated can strengthen his or her governing skills, thereby making a stronger contribution to the governing process. School boards that have invested in systematic governing-skills development have realized a powerful return on their investment, in terms not only of higher-impact governance, but also in strengthening the morale and commitment of board members. Many boards these days, for example, annually adopt a formal program and budget for development of ongoing board member governing skills, utilizing such elements as supporting education and training through attendance at conferences and workshops, building a board "lending library" of pertinent books and articles on governance that are circulated among board members, and assigning long-tenured board members to serve for several months as mentors to newcomers on the board.

How ironic it is that many board members we have met over the years have felt guilty about—and have often strongly resisted—spending time and money on developing their own governing skills, often offering the dubious rationale that spending money on the board would deprive students of needed services. You do not need to ponder at length about the critical role of your school board in setting educational directions, establishing educational performance standards, and ensuring adequate district funding to realize how penny-wise and pound-foolish this kind of board self-effacement is. Indeed, neglecting the need to develop governing skills among your school board members will over the long run cause serious damage to the educational bottom line of your district.

Board Performance Management

The evidence is overwhelming: boards that take the trouble to set clear, detailed performance standards and targets for themselves tend to do a better job of governing than boards that avoid self-monitoring. Like every other organization in existence, a board that takes accountability for its performance is highly likely to perform at a higher level. Board performance management basically involves two steps:

- Reaching agreement on the standards and targets that will be used to assess board governing performance, and
- Regularly monitoring performance, identifying shortfalls and corrective actions (often through a standing committee of the board)

If your school board is not currently paying much attention to its own performance management, then the intensive, day-long board governance design session that is described above can be an effective forum for identifying governing performance standards and targets. Thereafter, a standing committee (we later recommend the executive or governance committee) can take ongoing responsibility for this function. Performance targets for the board as a whole, which can be drawn from the board governing mission that is discussed later in this chapter, relate to the principal governing products and decisions in broad governing streams: planning and development, performance oversight, and policy making. For example, as a whole, your school board can take accountability for ensuring that the district's vision is updated periodically, that strategic issues facing the district are identified, that the annual operational plan and budget are driven by board agreement on major district performance standards, and the like.

We are keenly aware that setting targets for, and monitoring the performance of, individuals on the board is always a sensitive issue in school districts because the boards are either elected or appointed, and neither the appointers nor the electors typically put pressure on a board to manage its own governing performance. And, of course, school boards are typically mandated to take action against erring members only in extreme cases, such as clear conflicts of interest or conviction on a criminal charge.

An Accountable Committee

Later in this chapter we take a detailed look at board structure, focusing on the valuable role that well-designed standing committees can play in helping the school board to govern at a high level. Two of the most valuable contributions of standing committees are, first, dividing the detailed labor of governing into "chewable chunks," and second, strengthening accountability for performing particular governing functions. This is certainly the case in the area of board human resource development, and so an increasing number of boards around the country are assigning a particular committee—often the executive (or what we later recommend be called the governance) committee—the responsibility for this critical function. Among the more important responsibilities of the board committee are:

- Taking the lead in developing the composition of the board, including updating the profile of board member attributes and qualifications, fashioning strategies to influence the voting public or appointing authority in filling board vacancies, and overseeing the implementation of such strategies;
- Working with the superintendent in developing a detailed annual program and budget for board member skills development;
- Developing and proposing to the board for adoption performance targets for the board and for individual members;

- Monitoring the performance of the board collectively and of individual members and calling the board's attention to significant shortfalls.

DEVELOPING THE BOARD'S GOVERNING WORK

No matter how experienced, skilled, and dedicated the people filling seats on your district's board are, you cannot expect them to provide high-impact governance without mapping out their governing work in detail. In chapter 1 we defined governing as the process of answering—not alone but in partnership with the superintendent and the executive managers of the district—three key questions on a continuing basis:

- **Where is our school district going?** What is our vision, what are our strategic directions, what are our more specific targets for growth (or contraction) over the long run?
- **What is our school district right now?** What is our mission, what educational programs and services are we offering to the community in exchange for its financial and political support, what is our current revenue/expense budget, what performance targets are we using to measure our effectiveness and efficiency?
- **How is our school district doing?** How does our performance—educationally, administratively, financially—stack up against our self-defined and externally mandated performance standards, what are our strengths and weaknesses in various areas of district activity, such as leadership, financial resource development, and external relations?

MINING FOR THE GOVERNING "GOLD"

Updating the detailed governing work of your district's governing board to ensure that these preeminent governing questions are regularly answered in a full and timely fashion basically involves determining (1) the "governing products" that your board should regularly make decisions and judgments about, and (2) the role your board should play in generating and shaping these products, beyond making decisions and judgments about them. By governing product, we mean written items such as vision and mission statements, budgets, strategic issues, change initiatives, financial reports, and the like. Boards can help to generate some of these products, and they make formal decisions (such as adopting the budget) about all of them. By thinking of governing as making decisions about concrete products, we demystify it, bringing it down to earth and making it easier to develop consciously.

This process of mapping out the detailed work of the board can be most effectively managed, in our experience, in a one- to two-day retreat, which will allow enough time for board members to "discover" the answers and make the determinations themselves. Merely lecturing to board members about the work they should be doing is highly unlikely to generate the ownership or commitment required to implement significant improvements in board governing process and structure.

We are well aware that the proverbial governing train is already running down the track; at any given time, school boards are already busy dealing with the normal business—the inexorable flow of information and action items that fill, and often clutter, the typical school board agenda. As you read this section, you and many of your board members might be tempted to say, "We don't need to create more things to do; we're already up to our eyeballs in work. Look at the board packet we get every month—at least an inch thick, and we barely get through it the way it is!" We would have no reason to doubt your word on this, but it is essentially beside the point, for the simple reason that much of what your board is already doing—its normal governing work in terms of the existing flow of paper—is very likely to include an unhealthy amount of *low-impact* activity that could not accurately be called governing your district. For example, we have seen hundreds of board agendas that are cluttered with pro forma personnel, curriculum, and contract actions that are essentially operational in nature and are basically for-information-only briefings.

If you and your colleagues on the board really do believe in governing your school district at a high level, you must step back from the fray, rising above the inexorable current flow of action and information items, and ask yourself this key question: Whatever else my board might be doing now, what *should* we be spending precious board time on that really will make a significant difference in the life of our school district? This does not mean that your board can merely do away with nongoverning activity that is essentially operational in nature, such as acting on employment contracts; in our experience, much of the lower level work that school boards do is required by law. However, what you can do is ensure that the governing "gold" actually receives serious attention, while the lesser "dross" is dealt with only perfunctorily (for example, via a consent agenda). Mining for governing gold is what designing your board's work is all about.

DEVELOPING THE DETAILED GOVERNING WORK

Board governing products for the most part flow along three broad streams: planning, performance oversight, and policy making. In the area of planning, for example, at the strategic end of the spectrum are such products as values, vision, and mission statements and strategic change initiatives (see chapter 3), and at the more operational end of the spectrum are the annual operating plan and budget. In the area of performance oversight, we have the monthly financial and educational performance reports and the annual audit report. Policies are basically rules that govern operations in your school district, relating to management support systems (e.g., human resource management, contract management, financial management) and administration of the educational enterprise (e.g., promotion, grading, attendance, eligibility to participate in extracurricular activities). Rule making tends to be a very slight part of a high-impact governing board's work, for the simple reason that once rules have been made, they only need to be updated periodically. This is why describing governance as essentially policy making would be terribly misleading—not close to conveying the full richness of the governing process.

Once your board has reached agreement on the major products in these broad governing streams that merit serious board attention, the next step is to determine the extent and nature of board involvement in generating and shaping the products. In thinking through the board's role vis-à-vis these products, you cannot rely on a hard and fast distinction between "strategic" and "policy-level" products calling for more detailed board involvement, on the one hand,

and more "operational" products calling for slighter board involvement on the other. Rather, you and your board members will engage in a more creative division of labor on a product-by-product basis, with the aim of making full use of the board as a resource while not involving board members in work best done by paid professionals. The answers will come from a detailed, open, creative board–CEO–executive management dialogue, not from reference to clear boundaries. This dialogue can most effectively occur in a standing committee meeting, rather than at the full board level.

For example, you will certainly want your board to actively participate in updating such products as your district's values, vision for the future, and mission statement, perhaps generating rough-cut statements in an annual planning retreat, which your executive managers might refine and send on to the board's planning committee for further refinement and eventual adoption by the full board. Some products that boards make decisions and judgments about offer less opportunity for board involvement in shaping their content, such as the annual budget document and the monthly financial report. Even here, however, there is room for creative board involvement without meddling in executive matters.

Many school boards, for example, hold annual pre-budget operational planning work sessions after the annual strategic planning retreat and before submission of the detailed expenditure and revenue budget, at which the board, superintendent, and executive managers focus on anticipated operational innovations, major new or increased expenditures, and policy issues needing board guidance. Such work sessions can generate valuable board guidance in preparation of the detailed budget document (e.g., additional information needed on specific issues). And even though no board should be involved in generating a monthly financial report or an annual independent audit, it makes good sense for your board's performance oversight committee to work with the superintendent and executive staff in determining the format of the financial report to the board and the process for presentation and review of the independent audit. For example, many school boards these days are requesting the use of creative graphics (e.g., line graphs and bar charts) in the presentation of financial information, making it easier to understand and ask questions about financial performance.

THE BOARD GOVERNING MISSION

A sensible first step in the process of mapping out—and in subsequent years refining and updating—your school board's governing work is to develop and formally adopt a detailed board governing mission, which can serve as a framework within which your board can reach agreement on the detailed processes for dealing with key governing products. If the idea of a mission statement that is uniquely your board's sounds a bit strange at first blush, just keep in mind that your board is a particular organizational unit within your wider school district organization and can, along with every other organizational unit in your district, have a mission to guide its work. In fact, its governing work will be enhanced by having its own mission.

The first cut of your board's governing mission can be developed in the governance retreat discussed earlier in this chapter, refined later, and eventually adopted by resolution. The governing mission not only provides your board with a framework within which its detailed governing work can be fleshed out, but it also raises the sights of board members, drawing their eyes to the governing gold, and serving as a collective conscience that stays their hand when they are tempted to dabble in nongoverning operational detail. A well-crafted board governing mission can be put to other uses in the interest of higher-impact governance in your district: helping to attract qualified candidates for vacancies on your board, serving as an orientation tool for newly elected or appointed board members, and even strengthening board teamwork and board members' self esteem (solemnizing the work of governing, signaling that it is not just an amateur endeavor).

The most effective governing missions that we have seen over the years are divided into two parts: the desired outcomes and impacts of the board's governing efforts over the long run, and a more internally focused look at key elements of the board's governing process and culture (essentially the values that should govern the board's functioning). To be of any practical use in guiding the development and implementation of your board's detailed governing work, the governing mission also should be detailed, covering several specific points, rather than a beautifully crafted pithy paragraph of two or three sentences. Exhibit A in the next section provides an example of a well-developed board governing mission.

The governing mission provides your board with a broad measuring stick for looking at the board's governing performance. For example, take one of the meatier points in Exhibit A: "Plays a leading, proactive role in the District's strategic and operational planning, setting strong, clear strategic directions and priorities for all of the District's educational programs and administrative units." Merely making this statement does not automatically accomplish anything; it might be mere rhetoric—easily said, soon forgotten. But, if taken seriously, it prompts your board, perhaps through its planning and development committee, to ask some pertinent questions about designing governing work: What is our district's strategic planning process and annual calendar? Where in the strategic planning process does it make sense for our board to provide proactive input? What input can the board provide in operational planning that will help to shape the annual budget, without meddling in truly administrative details?

THE CONTRIBUTION OF COMMITTEES

Not only can you develop your school board as an organization by developing the people serving on it and fleshing out the work of governing, you can also develop your board's governing structure, which is basically a matter of defining the organizational units within the board—its "moving parts"—that will accomplish its detailed governing work. The major structural components of your school board consist of the board sitting in plenary session or as a committee-of-the-whole; the board's standing committees; and the board's ad hoc bodies, which by definition come and go. Experience has taught us that a structure of well-designed board standing committees can make a powerful contribution to high-impact governing, and so we conclude this chapter with a brief look at standing committees. Our intent is not to sell you on the use of strong standing committees, but rather to make sure that you understand the benefits that well-designed committees can generate and the key design features of an effective committee structure.

Experience has taught us that well-designed standing committees of a board can produce important outcomes:

EXHIBIT A

The Board Governing Mission

Our School Board, as the governing body of our school district:

- Serves as the steward and guardian of the district's values, vision, and mission;
- Plays a leading, proactive role in the district's strategic and operational planning, setting strong, clear strategic directions and priorities for all of the district's educational programs and administrative units;
- Monitors district educational, administrative, and financial performance against clearly defined performance targets;
- Ensures that our district's image and relationships with key stakeholders are positive and that they contribute to the district's educational and administrative effectiveness;
- Makes sure that our district possesses the human, financial, and other resources necessary to realize its educational vision and fully carry out its educational mission;
- Encourages the election (or appointment) of new board members who possess the attributes and qualifications required for strong governance and whose appointment will promote diversity in board composition;
- Pays close attention to maintaining a positive and productive board–superintendent working partnership;
- Ensures that board members are fully engaged in the governance process and that the resources they bring to the board are fully utilized in governing;
- Systematically develops the governing skills of board members;
- Promotes active teamwork on the board;
- Takes accountability for its own performance as a governing body, by setting clear board member performance targets and regularly monitoring performance;

- Above all else, standing committees can divide the labor of governing into "chewable chunks," enabling board members to delve into governing matters in greater detail than is possible at the full board level, thereby strengthening preparation for full board meetings and ultimately improving the quality of board decision making.
- In-depth committee work builds governing expertise among board members, while also enhancing their satisfaction and strengthening their feelings of ownership and commitment. Decisions that are the products of detailed standing committee work are firmer because of the ownership that is built at the committee level.
- Standing committees are a very effective venue for board members, the superintendent, and executive managers to determine the right balance between board and executive involvement in shaping particular governing products, in a situation where there are very few black and white guideposts and a large gray area for exercising creative judgment.
- Committees can also be a very reliable vehicle for building and maintaining a close, positive, and enduring board–executive partnership, primarily because the committee setting facilitates interaction at a deeper level than is possible at full board meetings, while also providing a more casual forum removed from the public scrutiny and higher pressures of the regular board business meeting. We are not, by the way, intending to suggest that standing committee meetings should be closed to the public, just that they will tend to be less visible and more relaxed than full board meetings.

When Committees Work Well

Over the years we have learned some very practical ways to ensure that standing committees really do function as powerful governance engines for your school board. The most important design feature of all is to ensure that there are only three to four committees that are organized along broad governing lines (e.g., planning and development), each of which cuts across all of your school district's educational programs and administrative operations. Organizing your board's committees along broad governing lines achieves the horizontal discipline that makes effective committee work possible. The polar opposite approach, which is notoriously ineffective from the governance standpoint, is to make committees merely a reflection of the narrower educational and administrative functions of your school district (e.g., curriculum and instruction, extracurricular activities, personnel, finance). This old-fashioned "silo" approach to committee structure inevitably leads to a board that is more of a high-level technical advisory body than a true governing entity and also, by the way, encourages board meddling in details better left to the superintendent and executives. Other important design features of effective committee structures are:

- Making sure that all board members are assigned to serve on one and only one standing committee, as a means to ensure that standing committees achieve a "critical mass" of participation, that individual board members are not overextended, and that governance is not thereby diluted;
- Requiring that items reach the full board agenda only through the standing committees, including not only action items but also informational briefings, and making sure that reports at board meetings are presented by committee chairs and members, rather than by executive staff;
- Building in strong executive support for the standing committees, principally by the superintendent's designating a senior administrator who is a member of the executive team to serve as team leader for each of the standing committees, responsible for working closely with the committee chair in developing committee agendas, for making sure of quality control for materials going to the committee, and ensuring follow-up for committee deliberations.

Board-savvy superintendents, in our experience, make sure that their executive teams are—collectively—actively and formally involved in supporting the work of their boards' standing committees. Many dedicate one executive team meeting a month to committee matters. At these sessions, committee team leaders review upcoming agenda items, executives discuss how to handle the preparation of materials being sent to committees, and particular high-priority items are reviewed in depth. For example, the description of a new educational program scheduled for transmittal to the planning committee for its next meeting—relating, say, to new computer software and hardware—might be critiqued by the executive team before being finalized.

We strongly counsel against your board's using ad hoc bodies such as subcommittees and task forces to deal with specific functions and issues (e.g., the tax levy campaign or the building of the new middle school) because such special-purpose bodies tend to narrow the board's focus, to detract from the broader governing functions, to overextend board members, and to involve them at an inappropriate level of detail. Rather than loading more baggage on an already extremely busy board, it always makes sense to utilize community volunteers on ad hoc bodies, working under the oversight of standing committees (e.g., the long-range financial support task force of the board's planning and development committee). Not only can this nonboard volunteer work enrich the governance process, it can also widen community ownership of, and commitment to, your school district. As we pointed out earlier, such volunteer bodies can also serve as a kind of board "farm system."

A MODEL COMMITTEE STRUCTURE

For a school board of no more than fifteen members, we have seen a three-committee structure work very effectively: two "meat-and-potatoes" committees to handle the preeminent governing functions—planning and development, performance oversight and evaluation, and one focusing on development and management of the board itself and on the board-superintendent partnership. The board's planning and development committee is responsible for paying detailed attention to board involvement in making all strategic and operational planning decisions—educational, administrative, financial—from values and vision update at the most strategic, to adoption of the annual budget at the most operational. Budget preparation is, of course, a pure planning function and should, therefore, never be assigned to a so-called finance committee. Budget control is a financial management function, on the other hand. The planning and development committee would design and host the annual board–superintendent–executive team strategic planning retreat and review and recommend board action on key planning products, such as the updated mission statement.

While the planning and development committee focuses on the next academic year and beyond, the performance oversight and evaluation committee focuses on what is happening now and what has happened in the past, paying close attention to monitoring educational, administrative, and financial performance reports and reviewing longer-term evaluations of educational effectiveness. In addition to its monitoring and evaluation function, this committee is often employed to serve as the board's audit committee, reviewing and recommending action on the annual school district independent audit report, to review and recommend action on operational items such as operational policies, contract awards, and faculty appointments that are already provided for in the adopted budget.

In recent years, boards have made good use of a committee—often called the executive or governance committee—that develops the board as a governing body, coordinates the work of its two standing committees, and plays a hands-on role in maintaining the board–superintendent partnership. Usually headed by the school board chair (or president), including the chairs of the other two standing committees, and increasingly often, the superintendent, this committee develops the full board agenda, ensures that the other two standing committees are functioning effectively, and resolves any questions related to the assignment of issues to particular committees. Setting board governing performance targets and standards and assessing the board's performance as a governing body are often handled by this committee, as is the critical function of board human resource development (helping to ensure that qualified people are elected or appointed to fill board vacancies and adopting the annual board governing-skills development program). This committee also often takes responsibility for negotiating CEO performance targets with the superintendent and conducting the annual superintendent performance appraisal.

In closing, we want you to keep in mind that, even if your school board is extremely small—say, only five members—you can make use of the concepts underlying the committee structure described above without actually creating standing committees. At the very least, your board's agenda can be divided into two segments: planning and development, and performance oversight and evaluation. Taking a step farther in the direction of dividing the governing labor without actually establishing committees, your board might meet twice monthly: once as a committee-of-the-whole dealing with two distinct agendas, planning and performance oversight, and the second time in plenary session to conduct the board's regular business meeting.

3

INVOLVING YOUR BOARD IN LEADING STRATEGIC CHANGE

STEERING THROUGH TROUBLED WATERS

These times are not for the fainthearted. The winds of change swirling around us—ever faster and growing stronger and more complex by the day—buffet our public schools along with other institutions in our society. Of course, that golden age of calm we remember fondly never really existed. Coping with change has been an essential superintendent skill since the beginning of public education in America, and successfully leading a public school district has always required extraordinary energy and ingenuity. However, today's always changing and often threatening world is uniquely challenging, forcing you, like it or not, to become a virtuoso at leading and managing change—not alone, but in close, creative partnership with your school board.

You really have only one viable choice in the matter. You, your board, and your top administrators will either learn to lead change or change will lead your district—very likely in directions you will regret. Whether your district will change in this challenging world is not a pertinent question; *How* you will change is. Will your change be timely, creative, planned, and well-managed, or will it be plodding, conventional, or thoughtlessly reactive? In today's context of constant, escalating change, superintendents who are enamored with yesterday's practices and wedded to the conventional wisdom will put their districts at risk of becoming the victims of change, rather than its leaders. *One of your preeminent challenges as a CEO is to help your district build the ongoing capacity to lead and manage change—systematically, creatively, and continuously.* Our aim in this chapter is to provide you with very practical, tested counsel in doing so.

OUR FOCUS: STRATEGIC CHANGE

Change comes in all kinds of shapes and sizes and can be generated in many places in your school district. Over coffee in the teachers' lounge, one of your math instructors brainstorming with an English teacher can come up with a creative way of teaching a mathematical concept that reinforces a grammatical principle in the same lesson. You can figure out in your Monday morning meeting with department heads how to handle an anticipated security problem at next Friday's football game. Your district's tried-and-true operational planning and budget preparation process can generate change; for example, you can provide in your budget for the upcoming fiscal year for a new language lab utilizing the latest in computer-assisted instruction. These changes are all important; they *do* make a difference, but they are not the subject of this chapter.

Our focus in this chapter is on what we call "strategic" change. In reality, there is no hard and fast line that separates strategic from tactical matters; the distinctions are in the eye of the beholder. Strategic change does not have to be grandiose or terribly expensive, and it can produce benefits in the short term. Without getting overly fancy and theoretical, we would like to propose a rough-and-ready definition of strategic change that has worked for many organizations in practice. *Strategic change is innovation that is aimed at dealing with issues that, in the opinion of your district's strategic leadership team, are strategic. We define a strategic issue as a major "change challenge" facing your district that (1) is in the form of an opportunity to move closer to realizing your district's vision for the future or of a barrier standing in the way of progress toward your vision, (2) involves high stakes for your district, and (3) cannot feasibly be addressed through the normal operational planning/budget preparation process because of its technical and/or political complexity.*

For example, the issue of a dysfunctional board is clearl\
definition. Not only are the stakes obviously quite high—ii
of eroding public confidence in the district—there is no im................... ....
issue could be dealt with through the operational planning process. It would
require special attention "above the line." Also falling easily into the strategic
category are issues related to a significant forecasted budget deficit, conjur-
ing up the need to raise taxes or to lay off staff, an influx into the district of
non-English-speaking residents whose children cannot easily be integrated
into your district's classrooms, and dramatic enrollment decline making it financially impossible to keep all neighborhood elementary schools open.
These and many other issues you can think of not only involve significant
benefits or risks, they defy addressing through the business-as-usual planning process.

THE GOLD STANDARD FOR YOUR BOARD

Making sure that your board is involved in a meaningful fashion in leading
strategic change will help to strengthen your working relationship with the
board while also producing significant benefit for your district. We think of
the process of leading change as the gold standard for your board's involvement in district leadership for three very compelling reasons: (1) the tremendous potential of change leadership to produce significant impact in your
district, enabling you to truly make a difference; (2) your board's capacity to
contribute in creative and substantive ways to the change leadership process;
and (3) the indispensable support that you need from your board in implementing "change chunks" (projects or initiatives).

Who can doubt that the work of fashioning and implementing change initiatives to address critical issues that your district is facing—above and beyond normal day-to-day operations—is both important and interesting?
When the issues are important, dealing effectively with them is by definition
important. Being involved in change management can be exciting and satisfying for board members, especially in the context of regular business meetings of the board, which, as you well know, can be pretty unexciting, and, indeed, often quite boring. The board member satisfaction that meaningful
involvement in a high-impact process such as change leadership breeds will

inevitably help to cement your partnership with the board, as well as building a kind of "CEO line of credit" on which you can draw when the going gets tough.

Board members are uniquely qualified to participate creatively in leading strategic change. They bring extensive, varied experience, diverse expertise, and different perspectives to the process of identifying, assessing, and rank ordering the issues facing your district, brainstorming possible changes to address the issues, and reviewing detailed staff-prepared change initiatives. Not only can your board members enrich the process of leading change, they also bring an essential resource: the power to authorize and legitimize proposed change, including the allocation of financial resources to fund change initiatives. As you have undoubtedly learned, the specter of significant change has a way of jangling the nerves of normal human beings, who very often respond defensively, resisting—overtly or covertly—change that impacts their day-to-day routines and takes them out of their comfort zone. Strong board support is very often essential in coping with such resistance.

TWO CRITICAL CAPACITIES

Successfully leading change in your school district or any other organization requires that you develop two critical capacities: (1) the capacity to *innovate*, generating practical change initiatives to deal with selected strategic issues, and (2) the capacity to *implement*, translating the initiatives into actual practice. We will explore both of these capacities later in this chapter. For now, we just want to map out the change terrain broadly. To begin, keep in mind that the capacity to innovate by generating change in the form of concrete initiatives depends on a marriage of two subcapacities, creativity and innovation-focused planning. Creativity, which by definition resides in the heads of the people participating in a change process, can be thought of as a kind of fuel that enriches planning. Its major purpose is to supply the *possibilities* for change. The more creative the people who engage in innovation planning, the wider your range of choice will be in terms of possible change initiatives. This obviously means that you can strengthen your district's change leadership capacity by strengthening the creative capacity of the people involved.

However, creativity alone will get your district nowhere in particular. It must be channeled into a planning process that is capable of generating innovation if it is to produce any practical impact. We need a planning process that will enable our district to identify, analyze, and select strategic issues and to fashion change initiatives to address the selected issues. However, even if we are able to identify and select truly strategic issues and put together sound change initiatives to address them, the journey from words on paper to concrete action can be a perilous one; witness the shelves groaning under the weight of unfulfilled plans. Rational planning and good intentions will take you only so far, and so designing the structure and process for managing implementation of the initiatives is a key piece of the change leadership puzzle.

BEYOND THE CONTROL BIAS

Over the years, we have been impressed by the powerful control bias of almost all planning that is done in organizations, including public school districts. Control of events and dollars makes the best of sense, otherwise things would fall apart in your school district. The annual operational planning and budget preparation process is the preeminent control device in the planning sphere. It may not be glamorous, but it works very well in keeping things under reasonable control. Programs are updated and refined, changing administrative requirements are addressed, dollars are reallocated incrementally among budget line items, performance targets are established. We put management information systems in place to provide board members and administrators with regular, timely reports on educational and financial performance. Not only does control serve a critical managerial purpose, in a tumultuous, ever more unpredictable world, but it also supplies important psychological succor, calming our very natural anxieties by giving us fixed points that we can count on.

By contrast, strategic innovation depends on the capacity to invent—to generate newness—rather than control. This means that, although the annual operational planning process can generate some innovation, it cannot serve as a vehicle for generating strategic change. Unfortunately, traditional comprehensive long-range planning, which was intended to be the answer to the pressing need for strategic innovation, has been a total bust as a change leadership tool, basically because it was designed to project everything an organization was already doing into the future, thereby enshrining the conventional wisdom for years to come.

To add insult to injury, long-range planning was often done for some totally arbitrary and meaningless period, such as three, five, or, incredibly, ten years into the future. Of course, since with few exceptions, there is no way of knowing what our future will hold much beyond a year or two, such long-range planning was never taken all that seriously, witness all the long-range plans gathering dust on the shelf, little if ever consulted once printed and bound in a handsome cover. And ironically, we have seen many organizations that have been heavily invested in traditional long-range planning make themselves strategically more vulnerable because of their investment. For one thing, this kind of comprehensive, document-heavy process demands tremendous time that distracts boards and executives from more strategic matters. Equally dangerous is the illusion of being in control that breeds complacency in a world demanding alertness and nimbleness.

Fortunately, in helping you to become a successful change leader and to creatively involve your board in leading change in your district, we can take advantage of a very powerful tool for leading and managing change, one that has been developed and thoroughly tested in recent years: the "strategic change portfolio." This variation on the broad strategic planning stream, which is the focus of this chapter, has emerged over the past fifteen years or so as an antidote to traditional, comprehensive long-range planning. It basically involves the leaders of your district in selecting the highest priority strategic issues facing the district and in fashioning very practical change chunks aimed at addressing them. Unlike traditional comprehensive long-range planning, the change portfolio approach is highly selective and action oriented. The point is to invest limited time and money in actually accomplishing some important change in your district over the coming year to deal with a few really serious issues, not to generate pounds of paper and thousands of words that merely confirm the conventional wisdom.

THE PORTFOLIO APPROACH IN A NUTSHELL

The annual bottom line of the strategic change portfolio process is the addition of change initiatives to your school district's strategic change portfolio.

These initi   ax increase pass   ended
to deal wit   am—
board, sup   attention. These   ugh a
process tha   udget
preparation   trate-
gic change   arate
from opera   s are
likely to be   strict
activities.

As the ye   they
are impleme   ed),

920-755-2376 • 1-800-950-7615 • Fax: 920-755-2186
E-mail: foxhills@fox-hills.com • Web: www.foxhillsresort.com
250 W. Church Street, Mishicot, Wisconsin 54228

and new in   own
unique time   tion,
nine months   t the
old-fashioned notion of a five-year cycle is nonsensical. When an initiative
has been implemented, it moves from the portfolio into the mainstream of
operational planning and management. For example, the revenues flowing
from the passed tax levy are now factored into the process of developing future years' budgets. The five elementary schools that have resulted from the
consolidation process now submit their annual budgets as part of the operational planning process. Meanwhile, the portfolio—serving as a kind of
strategic holding pen for your district—picks up new initiatives, each with its
own unique projected life span, from origin to implementation and ultimate
mainstreaming.

The strategic change portfolio process involves your district's strategic
leadership team going through the following steps:

- Updating your district's values and vision for the future;
- Identifying strategic issues facing your district—in the form of major
  opportunities to narrow the gap between your district's current situation and its vision and of major barriers or threats standing in the way
  of your making progress toward the vision;
- Analyzing and selecting the strategic issues meriting attention in the
  near-term;

- | .. issues;
- Adding these initiatives to your district's strategic change portfolio, where managing their implementation is kept separate from day-to-day operations.

We will examine each of these steps in some detail in the following pages, paying closest attention to the first three steps, which by their nature call for heavy top-down involvement of your board, superintendent, and senior administrators. Indeed, it is important to keep in mind that while the annual operational planning and budget preparation lends itself to a bottom-up form of participation, the much more selective and vision-driven change portfolio process is heavily top-down in form, even though your district can employ extensive participation in fashioning strategic change initiatives.

It is also important to keep in mind that we are essentially talking about two planning processes with a common beginning that are run side-by-side, in parallel, rather than the old-fashioned notion of strategic planning serving as an anteroom or umbrella for operational planning. As we discuss below, the common beginning is a board–superintendent–senior administrative retreat, at which values and vision are updated, issues are identified and analyzed, and guidance for operational planning and budget preparation is fashioned. After the retreat, the strategic change and operational planning streams flow in parallel. For example, as a superintendent, in the same week you might wear two hats: on Tuesday afternoon, meeting with your executive team for three hours to review preliminary change targets that have been developed by the task force established to fashion strategic change initiatives dealing with the district's projected deficit; on Friday morning, meeting with your executive assistant to go over the superintendent's office budget for the coming year.

THE ANNUAL STRATEGIC WORK SESSION

We made the point in chapter 1 that one of the more reliable ways of frustrating and alienating your board members is to hand them a finished tome to thumb through and react to. One of the reasons why traditional long-range planning became so unpopular with boards is that they were so often

These initiatives are very practical projects (e.g., to get the property tax increase passed or to consolidate seven elementary schools into five) intended to deal with strategic issues that your district's strategic leadership team—board, superintendent, top executives—have selected for near-term attention. These high-level change initiatives or projects are developed through a process that is separate from the normal operational planning and budget preparation process, and, once developed, are kept in your district's strategic change portfolio while they are being implemented. If not kept separate from operational planning and day-to-day operations, the initiatives are likely to be overwhelmed by the inexorable pressures of mainstream district activities.

As the years pass, initiatives drop out of your district's portfolio as they are implemented (the tax levy passed, the consolidation was accomplished), and new initiatives are added. Since each change initiative has its own unique time frame (e.g., forty-eight months to accomplish the consolidation, nine months for the property tax increase campaign), you can see that the old-fashioned notion of a five-year cycle is nonsensical. When an initiative has been implemented, it moves from the portfolio into the mainstream of operational planning and management. For example, the revenues flowing from the passed tax levy are now factored into the process of developing future years' budgets. The five elementary schools that have resulted from the consolidation process now submit their annual budgets as part of the operational planning process. Meanwhile, the portfolio—serving as a kind of strategic holding pen for your district—picks up new initiatives, each with its own unique projected life span, from origin to implementation and ultimate mainstreaming.

The strategic change portfolio process involves your district's strategic leadership team going through the following steps:

- Updating your district's values and vision for the future;
- Identifying strategic issues facing your district—in the form of major opportunities to narrow the gap between your district's current situation and its vision and of major barriers or threats standing in the way of your making progress toward the vision;
- Analyzing and selecting the strategic issues meriting attention in the near-term;

- Fashioning strategic change initiatives to deal with the issues;
- Adding these initiatives to your district's strategic change portfolio, where managing their implementation is kept separate from day-to-day operations.

We will examine each of these steps in some detail in the following pages, paying closest attention to the first three steps, which by their nature call for heavy top-down involvement of your board, superintendent, and senior administrators. Indeed, it is important to keep in mind that while the annual operational planning and budget preparation lends itself to a bottom-up form of participation, the much more selective and vision-driven change portfolio process is heavily top-down in form, even though your district can employ extensive participation in fashioning strategic change initiatives.

It is also important to keep in mind that we are essentially talking about two planning processes with a common beginning that are run side-by-side, in parallel, rather than the old-fashioned notion of strategic planning serving as an anteroom or umbrella for operational planning. As we discuss below, the common beginning is a board–superintendent–senior administrative retreat, at which values and vision are updated, issues are identified and analyzed, and guidance for operational planning and budget preparation is fashioned. After the retreat, the strategic change and operational planning streams flow in parallel. For example, as a superintendent, in the same week you might wear two hats: on Tuesday afternoon, meeting with your executive team for three hours to review preliminary change targets that have been developed by the task force established to fashion strategic change initiatives dealing with the district's projected deficit; on Friday morning, meeting with your executive assistant to go over the superintendent's office budget for the coming year.

THE ANNUAL STRATEGIC WORK SESSION

We made the point in chapter 1 that one of the more reliable ways of frustrating and alienating your board members is to hand them a finished tome to thumb through and react to. One of the reasons why traditional long-range planning became so unpopular with boards is that they were so often confronted with bloated plans at the tail end of the process, when there was virtually no opportunity for creative, high-level input. Many superintendents have found that a highly effective way to involve their school boards creatively and proactively in the strategic change portfolio process is an annual one- or two-day strategic work session—often called a retreat—that enables the board to provide input at a high level early enough in the process to make a real difference. Typical products of such sessions, which involve the superintendent and top administrators along with the board, are updated values and vision statements, a list of strategic issues that have been identified, and sometimes even potential change initiatives to address the issues.

You can take three simple steps to ensure that your district's annual strategic work session really does succeed as a kickoff event for the strategic change portfolio process:

First, employ well-designed breakout groups that are led by board members to generate content (e.g., the values and vision group, the environmental conditions and trends group). Breakout groups are not only effective vehicles for producing lots of information in a short time, they also enable board members and administrators to generate—rather than merely respond to—important content, which produces strong feelings of ownership. By contrast, merely presenting a vision statement at the work session that has been developed by the superintendent or a board committee and asking participants to comment would turn the board into an audience with little ownership of the content.

Second, do not attempt to turn the brainstorming that is done in breakout groups (e.g., the tentative list of strategic issues in the area of educational services) into formal decisions. Such seat-of-the-pants decision making is just as likely to do harm as good, based as it is on incomplete information and little time for analysis.

Third, build in a systematic follow-up that does turn ideas into eventual strategic change initiatives, for example:

- The superintendent and senior administrators spend a day following the retreat massaging and rank ordering the list of issues, coming up with the top three, which are then presented to the board's planning committee.
- The planning committee not only reviews the recommended three issues and determines whether to recommend them to the full board, but

also refines the values and vision statements for presentation to, and adoption by, the board.

- The planning committee and superintendent decide how strategic change initiatives will be developed to deal with each of the selected issues, and how recommended initiatives will be reviewed and acted on in the coming months.

Discipline is a virtue only up to a point. Experience has taught us that premature discipline is a clear and present danger in the business of leading change, primarily because change leaders such as board members and superintendents tend to be classic Type A personalities who are driving and impatient, wanting answers *now* and finding dangling ends offensive. One reason for employing a retreat with lots of built-in brainstorming and no decision making is to fight the very natural tendency to jump to conclusions, to get things pinned down, and to get cracking on implementation. Deciding too soon in the world of change leadership can mean missing major issues and making investments that do not pay off for your district.

THE STRATEGIC FRAMEWORK: VALUES AND VISION

Your school district's values and vision statements make up a strategic framework within which strategic issues are identified and selected and initiatives are developed for inclusion in your portfolio. Values are cherished beliefs and principles that are intended both to inspire effort and to constrain activities. They should be high level enough to provide ethical boundaries for the district. One of the most effective ways of developing a preliminary values statement at your annual strategic work session is to have a breakout group complete the sentence: "We believe in/that. . . ." For example,

- Attention to the unique learning needs and capabilities of our students;
- Active parent involvement in the educational process;
- Development of not only the intellect, but also the character, of our students;
- Education in social responsibility and citizenship.

You might think that, once developed and formally adopted, your district's values statement is now finished and need not be reconsidered, at least for another ten years. True, you would not want your district's strategic leadership team completely rewriting its values statement every year at the annual strategic work session, but taking a look at the statement every year and fine-tuning it does make sense. Not only do changing circumstances in your community now and then call for some wordsmithing of values (e.g., after September 11, 2001, being more explicit about the patriotic facet of character), but also newcomers to your board will feel little ownership of a values statement they were not involved in creating. And we strongly recommend that every four or five years you start from scratch in your strategic work session, crafting a new values statement without referring to the existing one. This will infuse fresh thinking into the process and stimulate ownership, and serve as a reminder that your board's planning committee can always follow through by reconciling the points making up the new and former statements, consolidating them into one new statement for the district.

Your district's vision for the future is truly the intelligence and driver of the strategic change portfolio process. A detailed picture of your school district's desired long-range future, vision is intended to assist in identifying the strategic issues facing your district while also serving an educational and inspirational purpose. Because of your district's detailed vision for the future, you have a gap between your district's current situation—its educational programs, operational plan and budget, staff, buildings, equipment, and so on— and its vision. This gap is where you can find strategic issues, which are defined as important opportunities that your district might capitalize on to move it closer to realizing its vision, and significant barriers, threats, and problems that are impeding progress toward achieving that vision. Taking action by implementing strategic change initiatives to address particular strategic issues, therefore, is essentially a process of narrowing the gap between your district's current situation and its vision.

Without a detailed vision for the future, there is no rational way to decide which issues facing your district are truly strategic and thus might merit near-term attention. Without a detailed picture of the desired long-term future, you will have no reliable targets to guide your investment in strategic change.

To serve this powerful strategic purpose effectively, your district's vision statement must be very detailed. We are not talking about the popular pithy paragraph of two or three sentences that you frame and hang on the wall. That is a summary vision that is explicitly intended to serve as a public relations tool and as a means for rallying the troops. We are not saying that your district should not produce such an abbreviated vision and such related public information tools as a slogan and a logo, just that in summary form your district's vision will not help you to identify and select strategic issues that you might tackle.

Your district's strategic leadership team can take a first crack at this during your annual strategic work session by assigning breakout groups to answer three key questions: (1) What long-term outcomes/impacts do we want our school district to produce over the long run? (2) What role do we envision our school district playing in the community over the long run? (3) What do we want our school district to be like internally as an organization over the long run? We encourage you to develop as long a list of elements as you can answering these three questions in the work session, subsequently cleaning up and refining the list (and eventually even producing a pithy paragraph version for public relations purposes). Some examples from real-life vision statements follow:

As a result of our school district's efforts:

- The great majority of our graduates continue their education at the postsecondary level.
- Our graduates are public-spirited and contribute in diverse ways to developing the quality of life in their communities.
- Our graduates are lifelong learners.
- The residents of our community value education highly.
- The residents of our community understand and are committed to the work of our school district.
- Parental involvement in the schools flourishes at all grade levels.
- Our community is a more attractive place to live.
- Property values in our community are maintained and enhanced.

Our school district aspires to be:

- An innovator in employing new techniques, methodologies, and technologies to achieve our educational goals more fully;

- An active partner with local government and civic organizations in strengthening the quality of life in our community;
- An organization that attracts and retains top-quality faculty members, administrators, and staff;
- A nurturing environment that systematically develops the skills of its employees.

Not only can your district's vision statement assist in identifying and selecting strategic issues, it can also become a valuable tool in the operational planning process. You and your board, for example, might ask the heads of your district's major administrative units (e.g., curriculum and instruction, pupil services, athletics) to explicitly address in their proposed operational plans and budget for the coming year how they are dealing with pertinent elements of the district's vision statement. Having been refined and finalized by your board's planning committee, and adopted by the full board, your district's vision statement can also be used—perhaps in concise paragraph form—to inform parents, students, and the general public of what your district's ultimate purposes are.

SELECTING STRATEGIC ISSUES

You will recall that strategic issues are change challenges in the form of opportunities to move toward particular elements of your district's vision, and barriers impeding progress in translating particular vision elements into reality. What makes the issues strategic are (1) the high stakes involved (educationally, financially, administratively, politically), and (2) their being too complex to handle through the normal operational planning and budget process. Strategic issues ask the question: Should our district take action—produce change—to address this particular opportunity or barrier? You and your colleagues on the strategic leadership team can surface issues in your annual strategic work session by brainstorming in two streams in the context of your updated (albeit rough and preliminary) vision statement: external environmental conditions and trends (federal and state legislation and regulations affecting your district; social, demographic, and economic trends in your community; technological advances with implications for your educational services), and an internal assessment of strengths and weaknesses (along such lines as educational performance, leadership—primarily board and superintendent, financial condition, and image/public relations).

Strategic issues can come in all shapes and sizes relating to student needs (a proliferation of single-parent families in the district, an influx of non-English-speaking students, an epidemic of teen pregnancies), educational performance (serious underachievement as measured by scores on standardized tests, high absenteeism rate in particular grade levels), leadership (a badly frayed board–superintendent working relationship), finances (expenditures forecast to exceed revenues three years hence unless action is taken), and the external world (lots of talk at the chamber of commerce about the need to work closely with your district in boosting student graduation and college-going rates, a new state grant program to fund experiments in computer-assisted instruction), and more.

We have seen strategic leadership teams of school districts come up with fifteen or more of these change challenges over the course of a day or more together in a retreat setting. Of course, if the process stopped at this point, the only product would be an interesting shopping list of opportunities and problems. The essential next step in the strategic change portfolio process is to choose the particular issues that will be addressed during the coming year—by developing strategic change initiatives that will be added to your district's change portfolio, where implementation will be managed. Selectivity is essential because your district can come up with only so much time and money to implement change during the coming year, above and beyond carrying out the day-to-day work of your district. Although General Electric or IBM can set aside hundreds of millions of dollars for innovation through dedicated research and development units, we doubt that there are many, if any, school districts in the country that have even a million in flexible dollars waiting to be used for innovation.

So how can you pare the long list down to three or four issues that you can afford to address in the coming months? We have found that the superintendent and her or his top administrators, sitting as your district's executive team, can do much of the job in an intensive day-long work session following up on the strategic leadership team retreat by employing the following methodology. Although it is far from scientific, the process is logical and, if seriously applied, can result in the rational choice of issues:

1. Take out the issues that, on closer examination, can be handled by feeding them into the mainstream operational planning/budget preparation process now getting under way.
2. Then analyze each of the remaining issues by asking:

- What will be the probable cost to our district if we do *not* take action on the issue over the coming year, in terms of lost benefit, out-of-pocket dollars, damaged reputation, and so on?
- What will be the probable cost to our district in tackling the issue, in time and money?
- What is our district's capacity to handle the issue (to come up with the time, dollars, and expertise that are likely to be required)?

Your executive team will obviously have to do some educated guessing in conducting this analysis; you cannot pin down precise benefits and costs before getting into the detailed action planning that produces change initiatives. However, in practice this has proved to be a pretty reliable means for whittling the shopping list of issues down to a select few that would provide your district with the best benefit/cost ratios. Some issues literally select themselves, because the cost of *not* acting in the near term would be astronomical. For example, if you do not begin to address the projected budget deficit now, your district will almost certainly have to take draconian steps later that will be damaging to internal morale and public confidence, steps such as eliminating music, art, and varsity athletics, or even arriving at technical bankruptcy and likely state receivership. If your district does not take action now to address the board–superintendent rift, the coming year will almost certainly see a number of stressful board meetings that would damage your district's reputation and lead to a final and very expensive parting of the ways.

The majority of issues will be less dramatic, for example: Do we take advantage of the opportunity to build a close working partnership with the chamber of commerce? Do we launch an initiative to deal with the special needs of students from single parent families? Do we mobilize a task force to secure the new state grant for computer-assisted instruction? In the netherworld of the "maybe" issues, the cost of not acting now is not dramatic enough to decide the question by itself, and so we (1) determine if deferring action for a year or more will make any real difference, and (2) pay more attention to the cost that the district is likely to incur by acting (as contrasted to the cost of deferring action). The objective here is to come up with a short list of issues that offer your district the most favorable benefit/cost ratios—the most "bang for the buck."

Of course, the benefits that might be lost by not acting will seldom be precisely quantifiable, and so your executive team will still be making largely subjective judgments that will often relate to values and philosophy. For example, your executive team might decide that—all other considerations aside—tackling the special needs of students from single-parent families outweighs initiating a joint venture with the local Chamber because the direct welfare of students always tops the list.

Since the judgments about what strategic issues to tackle during a given year are clearly high level, involving high stakes and requiring the allocation of precious, all-too-scarce resources, it makes good sense to involve your board's planning committee intensively in the decision-making process. At the very least, you will want the planning committee to devote one or two half-day work sessions to going over the analysis and recommendations of your executive team before reaching consensus on the issues to be addressed. Once this decision is made, you will want the planning committee to reach agreement on which standing committees of the board will provide general oversight during the process of fashioning strategic change initiatives. For example, the board's planning committee would naturally oversee the development of initiatives to deal with the at-risk student and the computer-assisted instruction issues, while the executive committee would naturally oversee the board–superintendent relationship issue and the external affairs committee the tax levy and chamber partnership issues. At this point, your board's in-depth involvement in the strategic change portfolio process has come to an end.

FASHIONING AND IMPLEMENTING CHANGE INITIATIVES

Under the general oversight of the appropriate board standing committees, you can employ various mechanisms for coming up with proposed strategic change initiatives to address the selected issues. The tried-and-true method is an ad hoc task force, which is phased out once its recommended initiative(s) has been reviewed and adopted by your school board. When an issue has a large external dimension, meaning that successfully addressing it is highly likely to demand in-depth input, understanding, and support from outside stakeholders, you will probably want to involve stakeholder representatives along with staff in the task force that will fashion the change initiatives. For example, passing a tax increase or building a strong partnership with the city government or chamber are issues calling for outside participation. It will make the best of sense to involve parents and perhaps outside professionals in the task force that is established to deal with the special needs of at-risk students. By contrast, a purely in-house approach would make sense in dealing with educational technologies, such as computer-assisted instruction, and with questions related to governance and the board–superintendent partnership.

The power of the strategic change portfolio approach lies in the selection of the right issues to tackle in any given year, not in strategy formulation, which basically involves the kind of project planning that is familiar to the great majority of professionals. Although the format of the particular strategic change initiatives will vary from issue to issue, they will typically consist of

- A detailed analysis of the issue, breaking it down into its sub-issues so that it is more "attackable";
- The specific targets that the initiative is intended to achieve;
- A detailed action strategy, spelling out specific tasks that need to be performed, accountabilities, and deadlines;
- A revenue/expenditure budget.

For example, let's say that your district has created a task force to deal with the issue of your district's image in the community, which is perceived to have become dangerously vague and negative over the years, especially with the dramatic increase in childless households. The task force has gotten a firmer handle on the issue by doing some survey research and running a number of focus groups. The sub-issues that have emerged from this research phase include lack of public understanding of district financing and of the district's contribution to the community's economy; a widespread perception that the district is elitist, in the sense that the educators running things know far better than parents and other taxpayers what the district should be doing; and badly frayed relationships with two preeminent district stakeholders, the city government and the parks and recreation commission.

The targets that the task force has come up with include an updated district image that clearly identifies the major messages that the district wants to get across to the wider community, an aggressive public information campaign making clear the district's philosophy and contributions to the community's social and economic well-being, and focused initiatives to strengthen ties with selected key stakeholders. Action steps include drafting the updated image and securing the board's approval; developing a graphics presentation employing slides that can be shown in selected high-priority forums; launching a speakers bureau to book board member speaking engagements in the community; and holding clear-the-air sessions involving selected board members, the superintendent, and representatives of key stakeholder organizations.

When the appropriate standing committee of your board—in this case, external relations—reviews the recommended image enhancement initiative, it should explicitly decide what level of resource commitment it will recommend to the full board to ensure that the initiative is implemented in a full and timely fashion. Without the firm commitment of resources, a strategic initiative is likely to remain rhetoric rather than being translated into action. Once an initiative is added to your district's strategic change portfolio and implementation begins, you will want to make sure that progress is rigorously monitored, separately from normal day-to-day operations. In this regard, two tactics have worked very effectively in our experience: (1) dedicating regular meetings of the executive team—the superintendent and his or her top administrators—to reviewing implementation progress and resolving any problems that have occurred, with no other matters on the agenda; and (2) segregating progress reports on strategic change initiatives from other performance reporting in standing committee and full board meeting agendas.

A CLOSING WORD ON THE BUDGET

We pointed out earlier that there are opportunities for your district's board to participate creatively and proactively in your district's operational planning and budget preparation process, although it is not a source of what we call strategic innovation and change. No superintendent can afford year after year to confront a board committee, much less the full board, with a basically finished financial package weighing a pound or two that board members are forced to thumb through, raising random questions. This approach relegates a school board to such a trivial role that it is positively insulting and sure to cause considerable frustration, irritation, and eventually probably anger—all at the expense of the board–superintendent partnership.

The line-item details making up your annual budget are clearly essentially administrative in nature, not the stuff of strategic leadership or policy making and hence not the detailed business of your board. So what can you do to facilitate creative, appropriate board input into this critical process of putting next year's financial game plan in place? We would like to offer a well-tested solution to this problem: a board–superintendent–senior administrative pre-budget operational planning work session held two to three months after the strategic work session. Hosted by your board's planning committee, this half-day session is aimed at engaging board members and district administrative unit heads in a creative dialogue that is intended to generate board input before detailed operational plans and budget proposals are developed. This is most effectively accomplished by each unit head making a presentation, employing slides with bullet points to facilitate easy understanding, consisting of the following components:

- The mission of the unit, in terms of its major purposes and functions;
- Operational issues that need to be addressed in preparing the operational plan and budget of the unit (drawing on the earlier strategic work session), with the identification of questions needing preliminary board guidance (e.g., the need to beef up security at varsity sports events to deal with growing parental abuse and occasional violence);
- Targets for operational innovation during the coming year, with special attention to required new expenditures that will be requested.

When the points made in this operational work session are recorded, they provide a framework for review of the ultimate operational plan and budget of each major unit. Rather than scanning through the proposed package and asking random questions, members of the planning committee can ask administrators to point out where and how particular issues that were discussed in the pre-budget work session have been dealt with in the document.

KEEPING THE BOARD–
SUPERINTENDENT
PARTNERSHIP HEALTHY

A PRECIOUS BUT FRAGILE BOND

Effective education is all about relationships and the active collaboration and cooperation of partners—teachers and students, students and parents, teachers and parents, schools and communities, superintendents and school boards. One of your primary responsibilities as superintendent and CEO of your district is to play a leading role in building and maintaining strategically significant relationships, and the one that is at the heart of your district's strategic and policy-level leadership—and most critical to your effectiveness as CEO—is between you and your school board. How productively and harmoniously this precious partnership at the top of your district's organizational structure works, more than any other factor, determines the quality of leadership in your district, and consequently significantly impacts the success of the whole educational enterprise. Knowing this, board-savvy superintendents devote considerable time and attention to building and maintaining a strong, close, and productive working partnership with their boards.

By partnership building, we mean far more than your just schmoozing over breakfast or lunch or on the phone with individual board members, although informal interaction with board members is a useful tactic. Serious relationship building is a matter of creative thought, meticulous planning, and rigorous follow-through. School boards, consisting as they do of strong-willed and opinionated members, can be difficult partners to work with, and many if not most superintendents have probably wished at one time or another that their board would just go away and leave them alone to carry out their CEO role without distraction and interference. But as you well know, you could not successfully lead your district without the active cooperation and collaboration of your board, and so relationship maintenance is always at the top of your list of CEO to-dos.

Although a school board is formally the "boss" of its superintendent and the predominant partner in the relationship, effective strategic and policy leadership of your district depends on the superintendent's serving as a strong, indeed coequal, partner with the board. As we have attempted to make clear in prior chapters, as CEO of your district, you must be much more than just a cipher or "go-fer" who is just there to serve the board's whims. Strength, thoughtfulness and professionalism should be what a board expects of its superintendent/partner, and that will sometimes lead to conflict between strong partners. This chapter will help you to navigate the sometimes treacherous waters of this most precious of relationships, minimizing conflict while allowing you, the superintendent, to provide the courageous leadership called for in these challenging times.

Making a substantial investment in building and maintaining a solid partnership with your board will pay handsome dividends, not the least of which will be your longevity—professionally speaking—as CEO of your district. A really solid board–superintendent partnership will yield other important benefits to your district, including:

- Enabling your board to effectively play a leadership role that transcends strategic decision making and policy formulation, serving as the preeminent vehicle for expressing the collective will of the community. Informed lay control of our public and nonprofit institutions is a sacred principle of the American democratic philosophy, and without your board's vital service as representative of the community's will, your district's indispensable base of public support would inevitably erode, leaving not only the district but also you as CEO less capable of accomplishing your educational and executive mission.
- Effectively dealing with the most important issues facing your district, through rational, timely decision making that is based on solid infor-

mation. No CEO or board can successfully go it alone in setting strategic directions, fashioning policies, or deciding how to grapple with high-stakes issues; each needs the other as an active collaborator in the decision-making process.

- Ensuring that decisions are backed up by a firm commitment of the human and financial resources required to carry them out and the political support that is necessary to overcome resistance and other obstacles.

- Setting a leadership tone that breeds confidence among students, faculty, parents, and the wider community. Strong, positive, and harmonious leadership at the top of your school district signals to the wider world that your district "has it all together," and helps to build morale and to create an internal climate of security and calm.

All human relationships require constant, detailed attention to keep them healthy, but the board–superintendent working partnership— consisting as it does of generally ambitious, high-achieving, strong-willed Type A personalities—is notoriously fragile and erodes quickly when underplanned and undermanaged. Of course, if the relationship is allowed to deteriorate past a certain point, one of the partners—in fact, always the superintendent, since school boards do not typically fire themselves for dysfunctional relationships—must move on to other professional challenges, at a potentially high cost to the district in terms of damaged public credibility, internal anxiety, inaction on important matters during the transition to a new CEO, and the often substantial cost of finding a new occupant for the CEO's seat. This concluding chapter is about what you, as superintendent and CEO of your school district, can do to make sure that the precious but fragile bond with your board is strong, positive, productive, and enduring. We focus on eight critical elements of a successful relationship-building and maintenance strategy that you can employ as CEO of your school district:

1. Making a firm commitment to playing the leading role in developing and maintaining the working relationship with your board, making sure that the objectives and strategies comprising the board–superintendent partnership "program" are fully developed and executed;

2. Securing your board's commitment to be an active partner in maintaining the board–superintendent working relationship;

3. Playing a proactive, aggressive role in building your board's capacity to produce high-impact governance;

4. Annually renegotiating superintendent-specific performance targets and standards with your board;

5. Making sure that your board conducts a rigorous annual evaluation of your performance as CEO;

6. Doing everything you can to make governance a richer human experience for your board members;

7. Building a close partnership with your board chair;

8. Communicating effectively with your board members, caring enough to send the very best.

PLAYING THE LEADING ROLE

The unpaid volunteers serving on your school board typically have extremely busy and demanding professional and personal lives outside of their governing work as school board members; consequently, the affairs of your district can claim only a small proportion of their time and attention except at peak times in the planning cycle or when crises occur. Just getting through the board packet thoroughly enough to be prepared for committee and full board meetings can be a daunting challenge to the average board member. So it would be unrealistic to expect that they can be an equal, much less predominant, partner in building and maintaining their working relationship with you as their superintendent. The ball is truly in your court as the CEO. If you do not play the leading role in thinking through what the board–superintendent partnership should accomplish and how it should function on a day-to-day basis, the chances are good that the relationship will not stand the test of time. Abstract notions of good governance aside, you have a huge stake in the relationship's working well since you would be the almost certain victim of a breakdown in this most precious but fragile of partnerships.

The first step in taking accountability for the working partnership with your board is for you, as CEO, to make a firm commitment—not publicly, but to yourself—to meticulous management of the relationship, treating it as one of your highest priorities as superintendent. We suggest that you employ a device that we have seen work very well for a number of board-savvy CEOs: treating the building and maintaining of your working partnership with your board as a high-priority program, for which you, as the superintendent, are the executive director. Although your board, collectively speaking, is your codirector of the board–CEO partnership program and must be an active collaborator in making the relationship work, the program in all its glory will exist only in your mind and on your legal pad. As CEO and program director, one of your responsibilities is to make sure your board is engaged at appropriate points in program development, for example, that your board formally takes accountability for participating in maintaining a sound board–superintendent partnership and participates in identifying desired characteristics of the partnership.

Like any other program head, you are the primary architect and designer of this critical program, making sure that the outcomes that the board–superintendent partnership is intended to produce are well defined in your mind and that the strategies for producing these outcomes are mapped out in detail. Some outcomes that you will want the board–CEO relationship program to achieve will be more "public" in that they will require formal board commitment to play a particular role. Since you, as CEO, are not in a position to command your board to do certain things, you must put on your facilitator hat and, leading from behind, secure their commitment to take the desired action. An example is annual evaluation of CEO performance, which, as program director, you know is one of the most important ways of maintaining a healthy relationship with your board. Therefore, one of your program strategies will be to facilitate your board's making a commitment to participate in CEO evaluation (and also to make sure that the evaluation process is well designed).

Some objectives of your board–CEO relationship program will be more "private," existing only in your head. For example, you know that your board members, being normal high-achieving human beings, bring substantial ego needs to the boardroom, even though publicly professing only altruistic motives. You know what they need, no matter what they say, and as program director, as well as board-savvy CEO, your job is to ensure that their ego needs are met, without ever explicitly telling them what you are doing in this regard. So the holiday greeting card that goes out every December has all the board members' names on it, and the occasional good news about the district that is reported in the daily paper more often than not quotes board members, not you or your top lieutenants. As program director, you would be well advised not to say to your board members, "I know you've got giant egos, and I'm making sure they're regularly massaged," but they will know and appreciate what you have done for them.

As executive director of the board–superintendent relationship program, you will want to set aside regular, prime time for thinking about the relationship in detail, assessing how various facets of the relationship are working, identifying problems that might be developing, and determining how to avert them. One simple approach that we have seen work well is to set aside an hour on Saturday or Sunday for this purpose. Your focus should not be on upcoming action items on the board agenda or on crafting documents that are going to the board. Wearing your chief psychologist and chief facilitator hat, you are dedicating time to thinking only about the relationship and how to ensure that it continues to be strong, cohesive, and productive.

SECURING YOUR BOARD'S COMMITMENT

Although you cannot expect your board to take the initiative and to play the leading role in building and maintaining its working partnership with you as the CEO, the board must be a willing, knowledgeable, and active participant in the process. The great majority of board members, in our experience, recognize and accept this obligation, which begins with the appointment of a new superintendent. However, many boards we have encountered over the years have had only an informal commitment to relationship maintenance generally and have not reached detailed agreement on the functions that they must be performing to acquit themselves well as relationship managers (with the exception of CEO performance evaluation, which is universally recognized as a board job). Securing the board's formal commitment to the specifics of this role is one of your challenges as the relationship program's executive director. The most reliable means of accomplishing this is to make it an explicit part of the process of your board's updating its governing design (see chapter 2 for a detailed discussion of the design process).

As you will recall, the most effective vehicle for involving your board in thinking through its governing design is a day-long retreat. Your responsibility as CEO is to make sure that the retreat agenda explicitly addresses the board–CEO working relationship. There are three points where this examination can naturally occur. First, when a first-cut governing mission is being developed, you can make sure that the board's responsibility for maintaining the board–CEO partnership is explicitly stated as one of the mission points, for example: "We will actively promote and support the development of a close, positive, and productive working relationship with our superintendent." Second, when committee structure is being considered, you can put forward the idea that the executive committee should be formally accountable for managing the board–CEO working relationship and make sure that this function is spelled out in the executive committee's formal description, including most importantly (see below) responsibility for negotiating CEO performance targets and conducting the annual evaluation of superintendent performance.

You can also build into the governing design retreat a brainstorming process that employs breakout groups to flesh out some of the content (in very preliminary and rough form, of course) that your board's executive committee can use, after refining and formalizing it, in overseeing the board–CEO relationship. For example, in a recent retreat that one of us attended, board members, the CEO, and her senior administrators actively participated in breakout groups that identified the key characteristics of an effective board–CEO working relationship (e.g., "open, candid two-way communication," "mutual respect") and critical CEO leadership challenges and targets (e.g., "upcoming staff contract negotiations," "building stronger ties with the business community"). Breakout groups are, as we mentioned earlier, a very enjoyable and effective way of learning about a subject and the preferred alternative to being an audience for preaching and teaching about it.

PROMOTING AND SUPPORTING HIGH-IMPACT GOVERNANCE

Countless times over the years, we have heard school board members—in interviews, over lunch, at breaks in school board meetings—complain that "we aren't sure what we should be doing" and they "don't feel like they are really in charge of things or making much of a difference." If even a few of your board members are confused about their governing role or believe that they are not accomplishing work of much importance, their inevitable frustration and dissatisfaction will over time threaten your working relationship with the board. School boards are typically so small (rarely more than fifteen members and often no more than seven to ten) that it does not take many unhappy campers to sour the relationship. It stands to reason that one of your preeminent tools for relationship building with your board is to make sure that the governing work of the board is mapped out in detail and really does make a difference. This brings us back to the subject we call high-impact governance.

Our definition of high-impact governance, you will recall, is your board's making a real difference in the affairs of your school district by playing a leading, proactive role in making decisions that answer the questions: Where is our district headed over the long run? What is our district doing right now? How well is our district performing? In chapter 2 we discuss the governing work that needs to be done to play this role fully, and in chapter 3 we take a close look at the gold standard for high-impact board involvement in governing: leading strategic change. We do not need to travel this road again here, but we do want you to keep in mind that your playing an affirmative, aggressive role in helping your board to become a higher-impact governing body will be the single most powerful way of making sure that your working relationship with your board is healthy.

Board member satisfaction—and hence your relationship with the board— also depends on developing the governing skills of the people on the board, which we discuss in chapter 2 in detail. Just remember that even if your board's role and functions have been worked out in detail and formally documented and its committee structure is well designed and working as intended, new members coming onto the board are highly unlikely to know how to negotiate this new terrain without special help. Without exception, they will need a thorough orientation on their governing responsibilities and will probably need a good deal of coaching and mentoring as well to "hit the ground running" as board members. Therefore, another important way you can avert the kind of confusion and frustration that can damage your working partnership with the board is to ensure that a formal program is put in place for bringing newcomers to the board up to speed and that it actually works as intended.

SUPERINTENDENT-SPECIFIC PERFORMANCE TARGETS

A few years ago one of us worked with a superintendent who had been brought into the district with a mandate from her board to get the organization into shape from a business perspective. Over the course of three years, this was her all-consuming task, and she delivered—in spades. A new financial management system took advantage of state-of-the-art computer support to supply administrators and the board with accurate and timely financial reports that made monitoring the district's financial status far easier than when she arrived on the scene. The budget preparation process was significantly upgraded, new purchasing policies and procedures were instituted, and contract management was at last put on a sound footing. The ship was now in superb shape. However, just about the time the superintendent had accomplished much of what she had been charged to do, her working partnership with the board had become seriously frayed, and several board members were quietly—behind the scenes—talking about her possible dismissal.

It turned out that this was a classic case of changing board expectations that had not been articulated to the superintendent, who, as far as she knew, was doing exactly what she had been charged to do when she had been appointed three years earlier. To be sure, four new trustees (out of a total of nine) had joined the board over this period, but they had not made a point of questioning the superintendent's priorities. Her style was brusque, and she did not suffer fools gladly, but the board had never discussed the matter of style with her. Her preoccupation with internal administrative system development had left a vacuum on the external front, and some key stakeholders in the community were feeling neglected, including the CEO of an influential family foundation that had supported several school programs over the years and the president of the chamber of commerce, which featured the school district in its business attraction strategy. However, she had never discussed priorities in the external arena with the board. There were also rumblings of discontent in the faculty ranks because the prior superintendent had been far more of an educational philosopher than his successor, who paid little attention to the articulation of lofty educational goals. The board had never explicitly asked her to expound on matters of educational philosophy.

Stories like this are not uncommon in our experience, and they probably end unhappily in most cases, with the wounded superintendent being sent packing without understanding what went so wrong so fast. The problem is usually a mismatch between many board members' expectations as to superintendent priorities and performance targets and the superintendent's understanding of those expectations. This kind of dangerous misunderstanding can be prevented fairly easily. One of the most important ways to ensure that your understanding of your board's expectations as to your priorities and performance targets as CEO—and one of the keys to keeping your partnership with the board healthy—is to annually negotiate CEO-specific performance targets with your board. These targets are above and beyond the district-wide educational, administrative, and financial performance targets that are reset every year through the annual operational planning and budget preparation process. They relate to the superintendent's priorities as an individual and the CEO's use of his or her time, rather than to the whole school district.

CEOship is a highly complex profession in all organizations, including school districts, requiring that multiple roles be balanced: partner with the board in governance; educational leader; top administrator; district spokesperson and diplomat to stakeholder organizations. In the context of a rapidly changing world that presents your school district with a constantly changing array of leadership challenges that call for CEO attention, the superintendent's leadership priorities will necessarily evolve. Last year's CEO priorities may not fit this year's circumstances. If the board and superintendent take the time every year to sit down together to discuss the changing challenges and the implications for CEO priorities and to establish new CEO-specific performance expectations, no expectations gap is likely to develop.

We recommend that the board's executive committee be accountable for negotiating CEO-specific performance targets with the superintendent. Categories that have proved useful in this regard are:

- **Support for the board:** What are the superintendent's targets in terms of promoting and supporting more effective board leadership for the district? For example, will the superintendent devote considerable time to making sure that the new standing committee structure is fully functional within the first six months of the new academic year?

- **External relations:** What are the superintendent's targets in terms of promoting the district's public image generally and more specifically in terms of building ties with key stakeholders in the community? For example, will the superintendent pay special attention to repairing a frayed relationship with the local economic development corporation, which has become a vocal critic of the district over the past several months?

- **Educational leadership:** What are the superintendent's targets in terms of strengthening the district's educational programs to meet changing student and community needs and to capitalize on changing technologies? For example, will the superintendent become the champion of curriculum reform aimed at better preparing students to thrive in today's increasingly wired world?

- **Financial resource development:** What are the superintendent's targets in terms of strengthening the district's financial condition, including maximizing and diversifying revenues? For example, will the superintendent personally take on the challenge of building a nonprofit "schools foundation" with a board of prominent business leaders that will actively seek corporate and other grants to promote educational innovation?

- **Internal operations and system development:** What are the superintendent's targets in terms of promoting operational efficiency and building an internal climate that is conducive to fully carrying out the educational mission? For example, will the superintendent spend significant time in the coming year meeting with faculty in the various buildings, listening to their concerns and exploring practical ways to address them?

- **Individual professional development:** What are the superintendent's targets in terms of strengthening his or her professional standing and professional skills? For example, will the superintendent ask for board approval to participate in the six-week leadership development program of a major university this coming summer?

Now, having read this discussion of superintendent-specific priorities and performance targets, distinguished from district-wide performance targets, many readers are probably asking themselves, "Aren't they inviting the board to cross the line into purely administrative matters? After all, any self-respecting

CEO should be able to handle the allocation of his or her own time, without board meddling." Our answer is very simply: Yes, our recommended approach does cross a traditional line between "policy" and "administration"—but it is a misleading demarcation that can cause no end of trouble for boards and their superintendents when it is inflexibly enforced.

Keep in mind that, as superintendent and your district's CEO, you are your board's closest partner in providing leadership to your district, and you are the board's most precious human resource. Your leadership priorities are, without question, your board's business, and those priorities have meaning only in terms of the use of your time. Granted, you would not want your board members to begin managing your calendar, critiquing your time management skills, but at a broad level, they should be invited to discuss your broad allocation of time to key priorities. Otherwise, you cannot reach meaningful agreement with your board on CEO-specific performance targets.

For example, one of us recently worked with a superintendent who, in a meeting with her board's executive committee, proposed that she devote fully one-third of her time over the coming academic year to rebuilding faculty morale and commitment. Wearing her educational leader hat, she would personally facilitate faculty meetings in the different buildings, focusing on classroom issues and needs, and she would personally work with a task force of faculty that she would charge to address administrative support issues. She made clear to executive committee members that wearing her educational leader hat so prominently over the coming year would be at the expense of another priority, external relations, to which she proposed devoting significantly less time than last year. Particularly, she suggested that the joint school district–chamber of commerce initiative on business involvement in the schools be set back six months. CEO time allocation at this level, which often involves significant tradeoffs, is clearly not only your board's business, but in your best professional interests as superintendent.

Another line that is often too inflexibly observed when considering CEO leadership targets is the one distinguishing between *what* you intend to accomplish as superintendent and *how* you will go about accomplishing it. You have undoubtedly heard people say that a school board should focus only on outcomes and let the superintendent handle getting them accomplished. In theory, this sounds sensible. Who would want a school board actively involved in putting together your detailed implementation plans, much less shadowing you during the day? But in practice, you must be willing to blur the line in the process of reaching agreement with your board on expectations, because the what and the how are more often than not intertwined and inseparable, particularly where your leadership style is concerned.

For example, if one of your top priorities as superintendent this year—explicitly negotiated with your board—is to reinvigorate an administrative staff demoralized by major cutbacks resulting from failure of the property tax renewal levy eighteen months ago, you cannot expect to accomplish much by barricading yourself in your office, issuing written exhortations periodically. You will have to be out there pressing the flesh, engaging people personally, at least understanding if not really feeling their pain. The choice is between leadership styles—the *how*, but it makes good sense to discuss this *how* question with your executive committee when negotiating leadership targets, for four compelling reasons.

First, the style choice involves significantly different allocations of CEO time. Second, the choice really will make a major difference in terms of CEO impact and ultimate achievement of the goal: a reinvigorated administrative staff. Third, when you are dealing with leadership questions, which are far more a matter of art than science, you *do* need the advice and counsel of your leadership colleagues on the board. They are the peer group with whom you should be working out such questions. And fourth, such open and candid dialogue will help to cement your bonds with the board, signaling not only your respect for, and trust in, board members, but also your self-confidence and lack of defensiveness.

We understand that fuzzying lines that some commentators describe as hard and fast and nonnegotiable will feel dangerous to some readers. Welcome to the world of leadership at the highest level, where creativity and flexibility are far stronger virtues than mere discipline and the protection of perceived administrative prerogatives! Keep in mind that even though you might feel like you are opening Pandora's box when you engage in detailed dialogue with your board on the use of your time and the choice of style, you will put yourself in far greater danger by standing back, inside the boldly drawn line, keeping your board at a distance. Such standoffishness will not only make any agreement on CEO priorities and targets less meaningful and firm, it will also deprive you of valuable counsel and of the more intense interaction that would help to cement your relationship with your board.

SUPERINTENDENT PERFORMANCE EVALUATION

One of the most important functions of a high-impact governing board that takes seriously its fiduciary responsibility to the wider public is to regularly evaluate the performance of its CEO. Many boards, in our experience, do this critical job poorly, and some not at all. Some board members apparently avoid CEO evaluation because it feels negative and makes them uncomfortable, and others because they have no idea how to do it well. As superintendent, you cannot afford to let your board avoid evaluating your performance, or to do a shoddy job at it, because a well-designed and rigorously executed evaluation process is one of the most important keys to a healthy, productive, and enduring board–superintendent partnership.

Evaluation also provides you, as superintendent, with greater job security. If your performance is not regularly and effectively assessed by your board, you stand a far better chance of becoming the victim of shifting political alliances on your board or of highly subjective judgments that are not performance based. Merely urging your board to carry out its evaluation responsibility will not, of course, suffice. A poorly designed evaluation might be worse than none. We advise you to take the initiative in working with your board to put in place a sound process and to make sure that it is carried out as designed. In this regard, we recommend that you consider the following characteristics of evaluation processes that have, in our experience, proved very effective:

- **A standing board committee is responsible.** One of the more important ways of ensuring that the evaluation process is taken seriously is to make one of your board's standing committees accountable for making sure that the process is well designed and for actually carrying out the evaluation. In our experience, the board's executive committee makes the best sense because it typically is headed by the board president/chair, includes the chairs of the other standing committees as well as board officers, and is responsible for maintaining the working relationship with the superintendent. In light of its membership and its central leadership role on the board, the executive committee brings special insights and credibility to the evaluation process.

- **The evaluation is based on negotiated superintendent performance targets.** The problem with the functional checklist approach to evaluation (e.g., assessing CEO performance in carrying out such open-ended functions as "serving as a spokesperson for the district" or "strategic planning," employing a scale of, say, one to five) is that it trivializes the evaluation process, is terribly subjective while appearing to be precise, and more often than not misses the point. Objectivity—and fairness—can be achieved only by basing the superintendent's evaluation on the extent to which well-defined performance targets that are directly linked to the CEO's leadership role have actually been achieved (see the prior section for a detailed discussion of these targets). Whether or not the superintendent is "good" at public speaking, financial planning, or some other general function would be irrelevant even if it were possible to measure performance in the absence of specific targets.

- **The evaluation includes active dialogue over the course of one or more intensive committee meetings with the superintendent present.** The stakes involved in board evaluation of superintendent performance are so high, and the subject matter of CEOship so complex that the executive committee should commit substantial time—in formal session—to discussing how fully each of the negotiated performance targets has been achieved. To prepare for the formal session, each committee member should do an in-depth evaluation of the superintendent's performance in achieving each of the negotiated targets. However, given the complex nature of the CEO's work, the evaluation process should amount to more than merely tabulating the individual results and coming up with a summary document that is presented to the superintendent. Active dialogue with ample give and take is in order as committee members present their individual evaluations. The superintendent must be an active participant in the process, for both substantive and ethical reasons. It would be unconscionable for the executive committee to complete an evaluation and just hand it to the superintendent.

- **The focus is on education and growth.** Evaluation is not intended to be a negative or punitive process. Rather, it is a tremendous educational opportunity for both the board committee and superintendent, who can use the process to learn not only about each other's perspectives, but also about the nature of CEOship itself. If seriously conducted, the evaluation process inevitably leaves its participants more knowledgeable about the business of leadership. It is also intended to result in CEO professional growth by indicating performance areas that need to be beefed up. In this regard, one of the outcomes of the process should be explicit agreement on the steps that the superintendent will take to strengthen performance, the timetable for taking action, and the board support that will be provided. For example, one of us worked with a superintendent whose board agreed that if he were to make a greater effort to build ties with key stakeholders in the community, he should be able to hire an associate superintendent to oversee internal administrative affairs.

- **Formal consensus is reached and formally documented.** The executive committee should reach formal agreement on both the evaluation and the superintendent's follow-through action plan, and both should be incorporated in a document that committee members and the superintendent sign.

- **The whole board is fully informed and invited to comment.** Although a board as small as five members might be fully involved in the evaluation process, it does not normally make sense to involve the board as a whole in depth. However, it is important that, at the very least, the formal written evaluation and the superintendent's action plan to address shortfalls are shared with all board members and that they be given the opportunity to offer comments and suggestions.

MAKING GOVERNANCE A RICHER HUMAN EXPERIENCE

If your board members find their governing work interesting, enjoyable, and ego-satisfying, they will feel greater contentment and satisfaction, and the board–superintendent working relationship will be stronger as a consequence. Board member interest, enjoyment, and ego satisfaction obviously depend in large measure on the substantive aspect of their work (the governing products they play a leading role in producing), but they are also the result of your taking responsibility, as CEO, for enriching the human-psychological-dimension of their work as a board. In this regard, you can rely on two courses of action that have proved highly successful in practice: (1) making sure that your board members find ego satisfaction in their work, and (2) creatively mining the theatrical potential of the governing experience. So, in addition to your being a strategic partner with your board and your district's chief educational officer and top administrator, you need to don two other hats: chief board psychologist and the board's theatrical producer. The need to successfully juggle these multiple roles is one of the greatest challenges you face as a CEO, but the stakes make the effort worthwhile.

Needless to say, the typical school board member has a pretty large ego that requires regular massaging if he or she is to be a happy participant in the governing process. This is a normal characteristic of the kind of high-achieving people who make it to the boardroom, and one of your most important jobs as chief psychologist to the board is to capitalize on every opportunity to provide your board members with ego satisfaction. As you scout for these opportunities, keep in mind that school board members, along with the members of virtually all other nonprofit and public boards, receive no compensation for their very demanding and time-consuming work beyond reimbursement of expenses, if even that. Therefore, you should think of ego satisfaction as a very sensible (and quite affordable!) form of nonmonetary compensation.

Experience has taught us that two strategies will serve you well in providing your board members with ego satisfaction beyond making sure that they are engaged in serious governing: allowing them to share the credit—visibly, publicly—for your district's accomplishments; and actively engaging them as spokespeople for the district. At the simplest and least expensive end of the spectrum, you can make sure that your board members are featured in the district's annual report, that they are quoted in feature articles on the district in the local newspaper, that they are booked to appear on local radio and television talk shows, that they hand out awards to faculty members and students at ceremonial occasions, and the like. At the more elaborate and higher-yield end of the spectrum, many school districts and other public and nonprofit organizations manage a formal board speakers bureau, booking board members to make major presentations to important stakeholder organizations, such as civic associations in the community.

When you book school board members to make major presentations on behalf of the district in important forums, you must make sure that they are well-supported and fully prepared to succeed in this public role. Always keep in mind that a board member who fails publicly and suffers embarrassment because of poor preparation is very likely to hold you accountable and not soon forget the fiasco. One school district, booking board members to speak on their highly touted "Vision 20/20 Program," provided them with attractive slide presentations and engaging materials for distribution. The superintendent and her staff went even further to ensure a truly satisfying experience for board members, providing them with opportunities to rehearse their presentations before small audiences consisting of board colleagues and top administrators. Do not forget that it is possible to become a very successful business person and/or prominent community volunteer without having used slides in making a complex presentation before a large audience. In fact, as you probably know, the most experienced and successful public speakers never go on stage without ample rehearsal time.

Wearing your theatrical producer hat, you are well advised to take the initiative in bringing drama, excitement, and even fun to the work of governing, which tends for the most part to fall far short of glamorous, and in fact involves lots of plain drudgery (reflect for a moment on the reception your one-pound monthly board reading packet probably receives from board members: a shiver of excitement? Not likely!). Here are some tactics that CEOs have employed to bring occasional drama and excitement to their boards' governing experience:

- Adding spice to the monthly board meeting by spotlighting exemplary faculty effort, noteworthy student achievement, and innovative new programs—not in writing, but by having the faculty members and students appear personally;
- Making sure that the monthly superintendent's report to the board is not just a ho-hum recitation of district events, but instead is a more personal "view from the top" that reports on interesting CEO-centric experiences and activities, such as a major speaking engagement before a national audience;
- Adding drama to the annual board–superintendent–executive staff retreat, for example, by making sure that the planning committee's open-

ing presentation on conditions and trends pertinent to the district's mission includes handsomely produced slides that make use of creative graphics;

- Making sure that board members are regularly offered opportunities to attend state and national conferences dealing with educational and governance matters;

- Providing gracious social occasions, such as cocktail receptions, at which board members can get to know each other better and interact with other community leaders.

YOU AND YOUR BOARD PRESIDENT/CHAIR

To the extent that your board president is an active partner with you in developing your board's leadership capacity and making sure that your board truly functions as a high-impact governing body, you will be more successful in building a close, productive, and positive working relationship with the board as a whole. As you well know, this can be a daunting challenge not only because of the strong-willed personalities involved, but also the built-in need to clarify roles that overlap to some extent and are potentially competitive. In our experience, despite the occasional "board chair from hell" who forces you to take a damage-control stance, most school board presidents, like the chairs of other public and nonprofit boards, sincerely do want to acquit themselves well as leaders and do want to work in partnership with their superintendents. The best advice we can give you is to be creative and aggressive in partnership building with the chair of the moment, making the most you feasibly can of each relationship, in the interest of district governance and your own professional well-being.

It is interesting that a title that is universally used for the top or second-ranking full-time executive of a for-profit corporation—president—is given to the volunteer part-time chair of a public school board, while the very nuts-and-bolts–sounding, un-executive-like title, superintendent, is used for the CEO of the school district. This has probably encouraged some school board presidents to see themselves as more than just board chairs, adding tension to a relationship that is likely tense enough as it is, but the fundamental division of labor is clear. The school board president is chair of the board, in this capacity responsible for the functioning of the board as a governing body—in effect, the CEO of the board itself. In this capacity, the president chairs meetings of the school board and typically heads the board's executive committee.

By contrast, the superintendent, as CEO of the district, is responsible for all educational, administrative, and support functions of the whole shebang. The board president runs the board, the superintendent runs the district's operations. However, the area of shared responsibility is wide enough that you, as CEO, need to take the initiative in working out a mutually satisfactory division of labor that is clear enough to keep the two of you from butting heads (most of the time). This is the indispensable foundation of a sound board chair–superintendent partnership. The principal area of shared responsibility is governance—the work of the board itself. Although your board president chairs board and executive committee meetings, you, as superintendent, must play an active role in developing the board's capacity as a governing body, and you and your administrators provide continuous support that enables the board to produce strong governance.

The superintendents who, in our experience, have built the closest, most positive partnerships with their board presidents make sure that their presidents are active, visible leaders in board capacity building. For example, they make a real effort to ensure that their presidents are knowledgeable about the governance "business," by attending educational workshops with them, sharing publications, and just simply discussing governance matters with them. They include their presidents in fashioning strategies to develop board leadership capacity, such as holding a retreat to update the board's governing design. And they make sure that their presidents are visibly in charge of board capacity building, for example, seeing that the board chair is supported in playing a leading role in the retreat. In this regard, one of us worked with a very board-savvy superintendent who arranged to have himself and the board chair copresent a commentary on the school district's vision at an annual retreat. Seated on bar stools before the whole group, they commented—from their different perspectives (chief volunteer and CEO)—on each of the elements of the vision statement.

The second area of considerable shared responsibility is speaking on behalf of the whole district, both internally and in the wider community. Internally, board-savvy CEOs look for ceremonial occasions, such as the annual faculty convocation and graduation, where the board president might appropriately articulate board educational values and priorities. Board-savvy superintendents also know when to have the board president address internal forums, representing the board, in support of the superintendent's carrying out a decision or policy that will require extraordinary effort or encounter considerable resistance.

Board-savvy superintendents apply a clear rule for involving their board presidents in the wider community: within limits of their desire and capability, involve board presidents to the maximum feasible extent in speaking on behalf of the district. Even in more intimate settings, such as negotiation with the mayor on a joint city–school district initiative, a board-savvy superintendent will involve the board president if at all feasible. The ego satisfaction that serving as a public spokesperson and representative of the district brings is one of the most important ways of cementing the board president–superintendent partnership.

COMMUNICATING EFFECTIVELY

Communication is a recurring theme throughout this book. Without revisiting points we have already made, we would like to close with three pointers on communicating effectively with your board:

- **Be honest and open.** Your credibility in the eyes of your board members, and the level of trust in the relationship, depend more than anything else on your always telling not just the truth, but the full truth—the bad news as well as the good. Over the years, we have seen very few superintendents get into trouble with their boards by telling direct lies, but we have seen many superintendents lose credibility by failing to make an effort to get the full truth out, or by forcing board members to probe and dig to understand an issue. The board-savvy superintendent makes sure that board members are apprised of the full array of options available to them in dealing with an issue, that they understand all of the important implications of making a particular decision, that they are alerted to the potential problem that is buried on page six of the quarterly financial report.

- **Be pertinent.** Some of the best-informed boards we have ever encountered are among the weakest at governing. Information is not, in itself, influence. The *right* information—meaning the precise information you need to make decisions—is influence. As you well know, effective communication with your board is more than sending it pounds of paper; in fact, too much paper can detract from sound decision making. If you truly do care enough to send your board the very best governing information, you will think seriously about both content (is it the right information?) and format (is it easy to understand?). The classic case of terrible communication is the monthly financial report that is sent to many boards: columns and rows of numbers, page after page, requiring an accounting degree to decipher. Effectively communicating financial information means creatively summarizing, categorizing, and displaying the numbers so that your board can understand, without undue pain and suffering, exactly where the district stands right now in terms of actual versus budget expenditures for major cost centers.

- **Be timely.** There are two aspects to timeliness. First, make sure your board members have the information they need to govern—in a form they can easily use—soon enough to make well-informed governing decisions. For example, a recommended policy with the required backup documentation needs to reach the appropriate standing committee in plenty of time for committee members to absorb the information before the upcoming committee meeting. Second, board-savvy superintendents rigorously observe a cardinal rule of timely communication: no surprises, meaning that board members should be kept apprised of important developments so that they are not caught off guard and publicly embarrassed. Board-savvy superintendents pay constant, personal, close attention to this kind of communication, always judging when board members need to be briefed—whether by e-mail, fax, or telephone—on current events in the district.

5

KEEPING UP WITH YOUR READING

OVERVIEW

This closing section of *The Board-Savvy Superintendent* is not intended to provide you with a comprehensive bibliography. Rather, we want to point you toward important sources of information in the fields of governance and CEOship, and to share with you particular books that we have found especially helpful in understanding the board–CEO partnership. This is not an academic work, and so we have no interest in documenting or validating the points made in this book, which have been thoroughly tested in our professional lives over a quarter-century. Therefore, we cite only whereof we actually know, providing you with references that we can vouch for because we have actually read them and ultimately put them to good professional use.

The public schools business—like all other for-profit, nonprofit, and public professions, trades, and industries—is unique, but you would stunt your professional growth by focusing exclusively on works concentrating on public school leadership, management, and administration. We have both found over the years that the most powerful wisdom transcends particular applications, and so this chapter takes a two-tiered approach: citing general sources of inspiration and information that we have found truly powerful but also providing you with public schools–focused material.

IN THE AREA OF GOVERNANCE

In General

The premier general resource on nonprofit and public board leadership is BoardSource (formerly known as the National Center for Nonprofit Boards). Based in Washington, D.C., BoardSource has over the years published a number of very readable and practical monograph-length books exploring every facet of governance, including developing board leadership, the board–CEO partnership, the role of the board in strategic planning and financial oversight, to name but a few. Of particular interest are Doug Eadie's *The Board-Savvy CEO* (National Center for Nonprofit Boards, 2001); Kay Sprinkle Grace's *The Board's Role in Strategic Planning* (1996); and Maureen K. Robinson's *The Chief Executive's Role in Developing the Nonprofit Board* (National Center for Nonprofit Boards, 1999). The reader is strongly encouraged to make a modest investment in BoardSource membership as a very practical way of keeping up with the rapidly evolving field of nonprofit/public governance.

Recent books that comprehensively address the subject of nonprofit and public board leadership include Doug Eadie's *Extraordinary Board Leadership: The Seven Keys to High-Impact Governance* (Aspen Publishers, 2001); Mark Light's *The Strategic Board: The Step-by-Step Guide to High-Impact Governance* (Wiley, 2001); and Maureen K. Robinson's *Nonprofit Boards That Work: The End of One-Size-Fits-All Governance* (Wiley, 2001). Two interesting and useful books that are now somewhat outdated are: John Carver's *Boards That Make a Difference* (Jossey-Bass, 1990), and Cyril O. Houle's *Governing Boards* (Jossey-Bass, 1989).

Focusing on Public Schools

As all readers will know, the National School Boards Association (NSBA), headquartered in Alexandria, Virginia, is the preeminent resource on public school governance. NSBA's *American School Board Journal* frequently addresses various facets of school board leadership, and NSBA's bimonthly newsletter, *Updating School Board Policies*, contains in-depth articles on a wide variety of current and provocative policy-related topics. In addition, NSBA offers for sale a wide range of publications that are described at its Website, www.NSBA.org.

Among the many books offered for sale by NSBA, we believe that five are most pertinent to your becoming board-savvy. *The Key Work of School Boards Guidebook* (NSBA, 2000) provides a framework of eight key action areas that effective boards have focused on. Ellen Henderson, Jeannie Henry, et al.'s *Team Leadership for Student Achievement: The Roles of the School Board and the Superintendent* (NSBA and AASA, 2001) addresses the leadership roles of board members and superintendents in the eight key action areas described in *The Key Work of School Boards Guidebook*. Kristen J. Amundson, Ellen Ficklen, et al.'s *Becoming a Better Board Member: A Guide to Effective School Board Service* (NSBA, 1996) deals with a wide range of topics, such as school law, personnel, finance, curriculum, and public opinion. Richard H. Goodman and William G. Zimmerman Jr.'s *Thinking Differently: Recommendations for 21st Century School Board/Superintendent Leadership, Governance, and Teamwork for High Student Achievement* (Educational Research Service and New England School Development Council, 2000) covers a number of steps that the authors believe should be taken to develop and strengthen local school board/superintendent leadership. And Eugene R. Smoley Jr.'s *Effective School Boards: Strategies for Improving Board Performance* (Jossey-Bass, 1999) focuses on practical strategies that can be employed in strengthening school board leadership.

The American Association of School Administrators and Scarecrow Press, Education Division, have jointly published two books in the area of school governance that will be of special interest to readers who want to deepen their understanding of the board–superintendent working partnership: *Roles and Relationships: School Boards and Superintendents* (American Association of School Administrators, 1994), and Jack McCurdy's *Building Better Board/Administrator Relations: Problems and Solutions* (American Association of School Administrators, 1992).

IN THE AREA OF CEOSHIP

In General

There is not, of course, a field called CEOship; there are, however, two bodies of knowledge transcending technical management functions such as financial planning and human resource management that are especially important for a superintendent aspiring to be a board-savvy CEO, in addition to governance itself: leadership and strategic planning/change management. Highly readable and insightful studies of the traits of effective leaders include Warren Bennis's *Why Leaders Can't Lead* (Jossey-Bass, 1989); Max De Pree's *Leadership Is an Art* (Dell, 1989); and Howard Gardner's books that are written from the perspective of a psychologist who specializes in the creative process: *Leading Minds* (Basic, 1995), and *Creating Minds* (Basic, 1993).

A number of books that are not the ordinary kind of reading found on most management shelves nonetheless provide insight into the difficult and demanding role of school leaders. Richard Farson's *Management of the Absurd: The Paradoxes of Leadership* (Touchstone, 1996) provides insights on the complexity and often illogical dimensions of leadership. Two books that incorporate Eastern thought into the realm of leadership are Jon Heider's *The Tao of Leadership* (Banton, 1986), and Thomas Crum's *The Magic of Conflict* (Touchstone, 1987). Two other books that are "out of the box" and provoke the reader to look at leadership in new ways are Phil Jackson's *Sacred Hoops* (Hyperion, 1995), and Joseph Jaworski's *Synchronicity: The Inner Path of Leadership* (Barrett-Koehler, 1998). Jackson incorporates the lessons of his coaching and his own spiritual journey into leadership lessons, and Jaworski examines the meaning behind ordinary moments.

Well-researched biography can also provide valuable insights on the characteristics of effective leaders. Notable recent examples are Taylor Branch's *Pillar of Fire* (Simon & Schuster, 1998); David Herbert Donald's *Lincoln* (Simon & Schuster, 1995); David McCullough's *John Adams* (Simon & Schuster, 2001); and Edmund Morris's *Theodore Rex* (Random House, 2001). Autobiography, while it obviously has a tendency to be self-serving, can illuminate aspects of leadership. Recent notable works include Katharine Graham's *Personal History* (Knopf, 1997); Nelson Mandela's *Long Walk to Freedom* (Little, Brown, 1994); and Colin Powell's *My American Journey* (Random House, 1995).

The field of strategic planning/change leadership is crowded with books exploring various facets of this complex subject. Recent works focusing explicitly on applications in the nonprofit and public arena are John Bryson's *Strategic Planning for Public and Nonprofit Organizations* (Jossey-Bass,

1995); Doug Eadie's *Changing by Design* (Jossey-Bass, 1997); and Gerald L. Gordon's *Strategic Planning for Association Executives* (ASAE, 1997).

Focusing on Public Schools

There is precious little written about the superintendent's role as CEO of the school district, but some very useful and insightful books and articles have examined various facets of school CEOship. Gene Carter and William Cunningham's *The American Superintendent* (Jossey-Bass, 1997) covers the topic well. William Konnert and John Augenstein's *The Superintendent of the Nineties—What Superintendents and Board Members Need to Know* (Technomic, 1990), while a little dated, includes an overview of the relationship that remains relatively unchanged since the publication of the book. Another book worth checking out is Larry Cuban's *The Managerial Imperative and the Practice of Leadership in Schools* (SUNY Press, 1988). Cuban is a former superintendent and one of the more thoughtful observers of the superintendent's role. A more contemporary look at the superintendent's leadership role can be found in Paul Houston's recent article, "Superintendent for the 21st Century," *Kappan* (February 2001).

The American Association of School Administrators and Scarecrow Press, Education Division, have jointly published a number of useful books examining various facets of the superintendent as CEO and leader, including: Paul Houston's *Articles of Faith and Hope for Public Education* (AASA, 1996); Dennis Kelly's *Lessons Learned Along the Way: Survival Tips for School Leaders* (AASA, 1999); Jerry Patterson's *Anguish of Leadership* (AASA, 2000) and *Coming Clean About Organizational Change: Leadership in the Real World* (AASA, 1997); and Chuck J. Schwahn and William G. Spady's *Total Leaders: Applying the Best Future-Focused Change Strategies to Education* (AASA, 1998).

ABOUT THE AUTHORS

Paul Houston, who has served as executive director of the American Association of School Administrators since 1994, has established himself as one of the leading spokespersons for American education through his extensive speaking engagements, published articles and books, and his regular appearances on national radio and television. He worked in schools in North Carolina, New Jersey, and Alabama prior to serving as superintendent of schools in Princeton, New Jersey; Tucson, Arizona; and Riverside, California.

Doug Eadie, president of Doug Eadie & Company in Palm Harbor, Florida, writes, speaks, and consults on public and nonprofit board leadership and the board–CEO partnership. The author of twelve other books, including *Extraordinary Board Leadership: The Seven Keys to High-Impact Governance*, he has consulted with over 450 boards and CEOs. Before founding his consulting firm, he served as a community college senior executive, a chief operating officer of a community services nonprofit, and an ancient history teacher at the secondary level.